TERENCE RATTIGAN

Born in 1911, a scholar at Harrow and at Trinity College,
Oxford, Terence Rattigan had his first long-running hit in the
West End at the age of twenty-five: *French Without Tears*
(1936). His next play, *After the Dance* (1939), opened to
euphoric reviews yet closed under the gathering clouds of war,
but with *Flare Path* (1942) Rattigan embarked on an almost
unbroken series of successes, with most plays running in the
West End for at least a year and several making the transition to
Broadway: *While the Sun Shines* (1943), *Love in Idleness*
(1944), *The Winslow Boy* (1946), *The Browning Version*
(performed in double-bill with *Harlequinade*, 1948), *Who is
Sylvia?* (1950), *The Deep Blue Sea* (1952), *The Sleeping Prince*
(1953) and *Separate Tables* (1954). From the mid-fifties, with
the advent of the 'Angry Young Men', he enjoyed less success
on stage, though *Ross* (1960) and *In Praise of Love* (1973) were
well received. As well as seeing many of his plays turned into
successful films, Rattigan wrote a number of original plays for
television from the fifties onwards. He was knighted in 1971
and died in 1977.

**Other titles by the same author
published by Nick Hern Books**

After the Dance

The Browning Version and *Harlequinade*

Cause Célèbre

The Deep Blue Sea

Flare Path

French Without Tears

In Praise of Love

Love in Idleness / Less Than Kind

Rattigan's Nijinsky
    (adapted from Rattigan's screenplay by Nicholas Wright)

Separate Tables

Who is Sylvia? and *Duologue*

The Winslow Boy

Terence Rattigan

FIRST EPISODE

Co-authored with
Philip Heimann

Introduced by
Dan Rebellato

NICK HERN BOOKS

London

www.nickhernbooks.co.uk

A Nick Hern Book

First Episode first published in Great Britain in 2011 as a paperback original by Nick Hern Books Limited, 14 Larden Road, London W3 7ST

Copyright © 1933, 2011 Trustees of the Sir Terence Rattigan Charitable Trust
Introduction copyright © 2011 Dan Rebellato

Front cover photo copyright © Hulton Deutsch Collection
Cover design by Ned Hoste, 2H

Typeset by Nick Hern Books, London
Printed in the UK by CLE Print Ltd, St Ives, Cambs PE27 3LE

A CIP catalogue record for this book is available from the British Library

ISBN 978 1 84842 163 9

Terence Rattigan (1911–1977)

Terence Rattigan stood on the steps of the Royal Court Theatre, on 8 May 1956, after the opening night of John Osborne's *Look Back in Anger*. Asked by a reporter what he thought of the play, he replied, with an uncharacteristic lack of discretion, that it should have been retitled 'Look how unlike Terence Rattigan I'm being.'[1] And he was right. The great shifts in British theatre, marked by Osborne's famous premiere, ushered in kinds of playwriting which were specifically unlike Rattigan's work. The pre-eminence of playwriting as a formal craft, the subtle tracing of the emotional lives of the middle classes – those techniques which Rattigan so perfected – fell dramatically out of favour, creating a veil of prejudice through which his work even now struggles to be seen.

Terence Mervyn Rattigan was born on 10 June 1911, a wet Saturday a few days before George V's coronation. His father, Frank, was in the diplomatic corps and Terry's parents were often posted abroad, leaving him to be raised by his paternal grandmother. Frank Rattigan was a geographically and emotionally distant man, who pursued a string of little-disguised affairs throughout his marriage. Rattigan would later draw on these memories when he created Mark St Neots, the bourgeois Casanova of *Who is Sylvia?* Rattigan was much closer to his mother, Vera Rattigan, and they remained close friends until her death in 1971.

Rattigan's parents were not great theatregoers, but Frank Rattigan's brother had married a Gaiety Girl, causing a minor family uproar, and an apocryphal story suggests that the 'indulgent aunt' reported as taking the young Rattigan to the theatre may have been this scandalous relation.[2] And when, in the summer of 1922, his family went to stay in the country cottage of the drama critic Hubert Griffiths, Rattigan avidly worked through his extensive library of playscripts. Terry went to Harrow in 1925, and there maintained both his somewhat illicit theatregoing habit and his insatiable reading, reputedly devouring every play in the school library. Apart from contemporary authors like Galsworthy, Shaw and Barrie, he also read the plays of Chekhov, a writer whose crucial influence he often acknowledged.[3]

His early attempts at writing, while giving little sign of his later sophistication, do indicate his ability to absorb and reproduce his own theatrical experiences. There was a ten-minute melodrama about the Borgias entitled *The Parchment*, on the cover of which the author recommends with admirable conviction that a suitable cast for this work might comprise 'Godfrey Tearle, Gladys Cooper, Marie Tempest, Matheson Lang, Isobel Elsom, Henry Ainley... [and] Noël Coward'.[4] At Harrow, when one of his teachers demanded a French playlet for a composition exercise, Rattigan, undaunted by his linguistic shortcomings, produced a full-throated tragedy of deception, passion and revenge which included the immortal curtain line: 'COMTESSE. (*Souffrant terriblement.*) Non! non! non! Ah non! Mon Dieu, non!'[5] His teacher's now famous response was 'French execrable: theatre sense first class'.[6] A year later, aged fifteen, he wrote *The Pure in Heart,* a rather more substantial play showing a family being pulled apart by a son's crime and the father's desire to maintain his reputation. Rattigan's ambitions were plainly indicated on the title pages, each of which announced the author to be 'the famous playwrite and author T. M. Rattigan.'[7]

Frank Rattigan was less than keen on having a 'playwrite' for a son and was greatly relieved when in 1930, paving the way for a life as a diplomat, Rattigan gained a scholarship to read History at Trinity, Oxford. But Rattigan's interests were entirely elsewhere. A burgeoning political conscience that had led him to oppose the compulsory Officer Training Corps parades at Harrow saw him voice pacifist and socialist arguments at college, even supporting the controversial Oxford Union motion 'This House will in no circumstances fight for its King and Country' in February 1933. The rise of Hitler (which he briefly saw close at hand when he spent some weeks in the Black Forest in July 1933) and the outbreak of the Spanish Civil War saw his radical leanings deepen and intensify. Rattigan never

lost his political compassion. After the war he drifted towards
the Liberal Party, but he always insisted that he had never voted
Conservative, despite the later conception of him as a Tory
playwright of the establishment.[8]

Away from the troubled atmosphere of his family, Rattigan
began to gain in confidence as the contours of his ambitions and
his identity moved more sharply into focus. He soon took
advantage of the university's theatrical facilities and traditions.
He joined the Oxford Union Dramatic Society (OUDS), where
contemporaries included Giles Playfair, George Devine, Peter
Glenville, Angus Wilson and Frith Banbury. Each year, OUDS
ran a one-act play competition and in Autumn 1931 Rattigan
submitted one. Unusually, it seems that this was a highly
experimental effort, somewhat like Konstantin's piece in *The
Seagull*. George Devine, the OUDS president, apparently told the
young author, 'Some of it is absolutely smashing, but it goes too
far.'[9] Rattigan was instead to make his first mark as a somewhat
scornful reviewer for the student newspaper, *Cherwell*, and as a
performer in the Smokers (OUDS's private revue club), where he
adopted the persona and dress of 'Lady Diana Coutigan', a drag
performance which allowed him to discuss leading members of
the Society with a barbed camp wit.[10]

That the name of his Smokers persona echoed the contemporary
phrase, 'queer as a coot', indicates Rattigan's new-found
confidence in his homosexuality. In February 1932, Rattigan
played a tiny part in the OUDS production of *Romeo and Juliet*,
which was directed by John Gielgud and starred Peggy Ashcroft
and Edith Evans (women undergraduates were not admitted to
OUDS, and professional actresses were often recruited).
Rattigan's failure to deliver his one line correctly raised an
increasingly embarrassing laugh every night (an episode which
he reuses to great effect in *Harlequinade*). However, out of this
production came a friendship with Gielgud and his partner, John
Perry. Through them, Rattigan was introduced to theatrical and
homosexual circles, where his youthful 'school captain' looks
were much admired.

A growing confidence in his sexuality and in his writing led to
his first major play. In 1931, he shared rooms with a
contemporary of his, Philip Heimann, who was having an affair

with Irina Basilevich, a mature student. Rattigan's own feelings
for Heimann completed an eternal triangle that formed the basis
of the play he co-wrote with Heimann, *First Episode*. This play
was accepted for production in Surrey's 'Q' theatre; it was
respectfully received and subsequently transferred to the
Comedy Theatre in London's West End, though carefully shorn
of its homosexual subplot. Despite receiving only £50 from this
production (and having put £200 into it), Rattigan immediately
dropped out of college to become a full-time writer.

Frank Rattigan was displeased by this move, but made a deal
with his son. He would give him an allowance of £200 a year
for two years and let him live at home to write; if at the end of
that period, he had had no discernible success, he would enter a
more secure and respectable profession. With this looming
deadline, Rattigan wrote quickly. *Black Forest*, an O'Neill-
inspired play based on his experiences in Germany in 1933,
is one of the three that have survived. Rather unwillingly, he
collaborated with Hector Bolitho on an adaptation of the latter's
novel, *Grey Farm*, which received a disastrous New York
production in 1940. Another project was an adaptation of *A Tale
of Two Cities*, written with Gielgud; this fell through at the last
minute when Donald Albery, the play's potential producer,
received a complaint from actor-manager John Martin-Harvey
who was beginning a farewell tour of his own adaptation, *The
Only Way*, which he had been performing for forty-five years.
As minor compensation, Albery invited Rattigan to send him
any other new scripts. Rattigan sent him a play provisionally
titled *Gone Away*, based on his experiences in a French-
language summer school in 1931. Albery took out a nine-month
option on it, but no production appeared.

By mid-1936, Rattigan was despairing. His father had secured
him a job with Warner Brothers as an in-house screenwriter,
which was reasonably paid; but Rattigan wanted success in the
theatre, and his desk-bound life at Teddington Studios seemed
unlikely to advance this ambition. By chance, one of Albery's
productions was unexpectedly losing money, and the wisest
course of action seemed to be to pull the show and replace it
with something cheap. Since *Gone Away* required a relatively
small cast and only one set, Albery quickly arranged for a

production. Harold French, the play's director, had only one qualm: the title. Rattigan suggested *French Without Tears*, which was immediately adopted.

After an appalling dress rehearsal, no one anticipated the rapturous response of the first-night audience, led by Cicely Courtneidge's infectious laugh. The following morning Kay Hammond, the show's female lead, discovered Rattigan surrounded by the next day's reviews. 'But I don't believe it,' he said. 'Even *The Times* likes it.'[11]

French Without Tears played over 1000 performances in its three-year run and Rattigan was soon earning £100 a week. He moved out of his father's home, wriggled out of his Warner Brothers contract, and dedicated himself to spending the money as soon as it came in. Partly this was an attempt to defer the moment when he had to follow up this enormous success. In the event, both of his next plays were undermined by the outbreak of war.

After the Dance, an altogether more bleak indictment of the Bright Young Things' failure to engage with the iniquities and miseries of contemporary life, opened, in June 1939, to euphoric reviews; but only a month later the European crisis was darkening the national mood and audiences began to dwindle. The play was pulled in August after only sixty performances. *Follow My Leader* was a satirical farce closely based on the rise of Hitler, co-written with an Oxford contemporary, Tony Goldschmidt (writing as Anthony Maurice in case anyone thought he was German). It suffered an alternative fate. Banned from production in 1938, owing to the Foreign Office's belief that 'the production of this play at this time would not be in the best interests of the country',[12] it finally received its premiere in 1940, by which time Rattigan and Goldschmidt's mild satire failed to capture the real fears that the war was unleashing in the country.

Rattigan's insecurity about writing now deepened. An interest in Freud, dating back to his Harrow days, encouraged him to visit a psychiatrist that he had known while at Oxford, Dr Keith Newman. Newman exerted a Svengali-like influence on Rattigan and persuaded the pacifist playwright to join the RAF as a means of curing his writer's block. Oddly, this unorthodox treatment seemed to have some effect; by 1941, Rattigan was writing again. On one dramatic sea crossing, an engine failed, and with everyone forced to jettison all excess baggage and possessions, Rattigan threw the hard covers and blank pages from the notebook containing his new play, stuffing the precious manuscript into his jacket.

Rattigan drew on his RAF experiences to write a new play, *Flare Path*. Bronson Albery and Bill Linnit who had supported *French Without Tears* both turned the play down, believing that the last thing that the public wanted was a play about the war.[13] H. M. Tennent Ltd., led by the elegant Hugh 'Binkie' Beaumont, was the third management offered the script; and in 1942, *Flare Path* opened in London, eventually playing almost 700 performances. Meticulously interweaving the stories of three couples against the backdrop of wartime uncertainty, Rattigan found himself 'commended, if not exactly as a professional playwright, at least as a promising apprentice who had definitely begun to learn the rudiments of his job'.[14] Beaumont, already on the way to becoming the most powerful and successful West End producer of the era, was an influential ally for Rattigan. There is a curious side-story to this production; Dr Keith Newman decided to watch 250 performances of this play and write up the insights that his 'serial attendance' had afforded him. George Bernard Shaw remarked that such playgoing behaviour 'would have driven me mad; and I am not sure that [Newman] came out of it without a slight derangement'. Shaw's caution was wise.[15] In late 1945, Newman went insane and eventually died in a psychiatric hospital.

Meanwhile, Rattigan had achieved two more successes; the witty farce, *While the Sun Shines*, and the more serious, though politically clumsy, *Love in Idleness* (retitled *O Mistress Mine* in America). He had also co-written a number of successful films, including *The Day Will Dawn, Uncensored, The Way to the Stars* and an adaptation of *French Without Tears*. By the end of 1944, Rattigan had three plays running in the West End, a record only beaten by Somerset Maugham's four in 1908.

Love in Idleness was dedicated to Henry 'Chips' Channon, the Tory MP who had become Rattigan's lover. Channon's otherwise gossipy diaries record their meeting very discreetly:

'I dined with Juliet Duff in her little flat... also there, Sibyl Colefax and Master Terence Rattigan, and we sparkled over the Burgundy. I like Rattigan enormously, and feel a new friendship has begun. He has a flat in Albany.'[16] Tom Driberg's rather less discreet account fleshes out the story: Channon's 'seduction of the playwright was almost like the wooing of Danaë by Zeus – every day the playwright found, delivered to his door, a splendid present – a case of champagne, a huge pot of caviar, a Cartier cigarette box in two kinds of gold... In the end, of course, he gave in, saying apologetically to his friends, "How can one *not*?".'[17] It was a very different set in which Rattigan now moved, one that was wealthy and conservative, the very people he had criticised in *After the Dance*. Rattigan did not share the complacency of many of his friends, and his next play revealed a deepening complexity and ambition.

For a long time, Rattigan had nurtured a desire to become respected as a serious writer; the commercial success of *French Without Tears* had, however, sustained the public image of Rattigan as a wealthy, young, light-comedy writer-about-town.[18] With *The Winslow Boy*, which premiered in 1946, Rattigan began to turn this image around. In doing so he entered a new phase as a playwright. As one contemporary critic observed, this play 'put him at once into the class of the serious and distinguished writer'.[19] The play, based on the Archer-Shee case in which a family attempted to sue the Admiralty for a false accusation of theft against their son, featured some of Rattigan's most elegantly crafted and subtle characterisation yet. The famous second curtain, when the barrister Robert Morton subjects Ronnie Winslow to a vicious interrogation before announcing that 'The boy is plainly innocent. I accept the brief', brought a joyous standing ovation on the first night. No less impressive is the subtle handling of the concept of 'justice' and 'rights' through the play of ironies which pits Morton's liberal complacency against Catherine Winslow's feminist convictions.

Two years later, Rattigan's *Playbill*, comprising the one-act plays *The Browning Version* and *Harlequinade*, showed an ever deepening talent. The latter is a witty satire of the kind of touring theatre encouraged by the new Committee for the

Encouragement of Music and Arts (CEMA, the immediate forerunner of the Arts Council). But the former's depiction of a failed, repressed Classics teacher evinced an ability to choreograph emotional subtleties on stage that outstripped anything Rattigan had yet demonstrated.

Adventure Story, which in 1949 followed hard on the heels of *Playbill*, was less successful. An attempt to dramatise the emotional dilemmas of Alexander the Great, Rattigan seemed unable to escape the vernacular of his own circle, and the epic scheme of the play sat oddly with Alexander's more prosaic concerns.

Rattigan's response to both the critical bludgeoning of this play and the distinctly lukewarm reception of *Playbill* on Broadway was to write a somewhat extravagant article for the *New Statesman*. 'Concerning the Play of Ideas' was a desire to defend the place of 'character' against those who would insist on the pre-eminence in drama of ideas.[20] The essay is not clear and is couched in such teasing terms that it is at first difficult to see why it should have secured such a fervent response. James Bridie, Benn Levy, Peter Ustinov, Sean O'Casey, Ted Willis, Christopher Fry and finally George Bernard Shaw all weighed in to support or condemn the article. Finally Rattigan replied in slightly more moderate terms to these criticisms insisting (and the first essay reasonably supports this) that he was not calling for the end of ideas in the theatre, but rather for their inflection through character and situation.[21] However, the damage was done (as, two years later, with his 'Aunt Edna', it would again be done). Rattigan was increasingly being seen as the arch-proponent of commercial vacuity.[22]

The play Rattigan had running at the time added weight to his opponents' charge. Originally planned as a dark comedy, *Who is Sylvia?* became a rather more frivolous thing both in the writing and the playing. Rattled by the failure of *Adventure Story*, and superstitiously aware that the new play was opening at the Criterion, where fourteen years before *French Without Tears* had been so successful, Rattigan and everyone involved in the production had steered it towards light farce and obliterated the residual seriousness of the original conceit.

Rattigan had ended his affair with Henry Channon and taken up with Kenneth Morgan, a young actor who had appeared in *Follow My Leader* and the film of *French Without Tears*. However, the relationship had not lasted and Morgan had for a while been seeing someone else. Rattigan's distress was compounded one day in February 1949, when he received a message that Morgan had killed himself. Although horrified, Rattigan soon began to conceive an idea for a play. Initially it was to have concerned a homosexual relationship, but Beaumont, his producer, persuaded him to change the relationship to a heterosexual one.[23] At a time when the Lord Chamberlain refused to allow any plays to be staged that featured homosexuality, such a proposition would have been a commercial impossibility. The result is one of the finest examples of Rattigan's craft. The story of Hester Collyer, trapped in a relationship with a man incapable of returning her love, and her transition from attempted suicide to groping, uncertain self-determination is handled with extraordinary economy, precision and power. The depths of despair and desire that Rattigan plumbs have made *The Deep Blue Sea* one of his most popular and moving pieces.

1953 saw Rattigan's romantic comedy *The Sleeping Prince*, planned as a modest, if belated, contribution to the Coronation festivities. However, the project was hypertrophied by the insistent presence of Laurence Olivier and Vivien Leigh in the cast and the critics were disturbed to see such whimsy from the author of *The Deep Blue Sea*.

Two weeks after its opening, the first two volumes of Rattigan's *Collected Plays* were published. The preface to the second volume introduced one of Rattigan's best-known, and most notorious creations: Aunt Edna. 'Let us invent,' he writes, 'a character, a nice respectable, middle-class, middle-aged, maiden lady, with time on her hands and the money to help her pass it.'[24] Rattigan paints a picture of this eternal theatregoer, whose bewildered disdain for modernism ('Picasso – "those dreadful reds, my dear, and why three noses?"')[25] make up part of the particular challenge of dramatic writing. The intertwined commercial and cultural pressures that the audience brings with it exert considerable force on the playwright's work.

Rattigan's creation brought considerable scorn upon his head. But Rattigan is neither patronising nor genuflecting towards Aunt Edna. The whole essay is aimed at demonstrating the crucial role of the audience in the theatrical experience. Rattigan's own sense of theatre was *learned* as a member of the audience, and he refuses to distance himself from this woman: 'despite my already self-acknowledged creative ambitions I did not in the least feel myself a being apart. If my neighbours gasped with fear for the heroine when she was confronted with a fate worse than death, I gasped with them'.[26] But equally, he sees his job as a writer to engage in a gentle tug-of-war with the audience's expectations: 'although Aunt Edna must never be made mock of, or bored, or befuddled, she must equally not be wooed, or pandered to or cosseted'.[27] The complicated relation between satisfying and surprising this figure may seem contradictory, but as Rattigan notes, 'Aunt Edna herself is indeed a highly contradictory character.'[28]

But Rattigan's argument, as in the 'Play of Ideas' debate before it, was taken to imply an insipid pandering to the unchallenging expectations of his audience. Aunt Edna dogged his career from that moment on and she became such a byword for what theatre should *not* be that in 1960, the Questors Theatre, Ealing, could title a triple-bill of Absurdist plays, 'Not For Aunt Edna'.[29]

Rattigan's next play did help to restore his reputation as a serious dramatist. *Separate Tables* was another double-bill, set in a small Bournemouth hotel. The first play develops Rattigan's familiar themes of sexual longing and humiliation while the second pits a man found guilty of interfering with women in a local cinema against the self-appointed moral jurors in the hotel. The evening was highly acclaimed and the subsequent Broadway production a rare American success.

However, Rattigan's reign as the leading British playwright was about to be brought to an abrupt end. In a car from Stratford to London, early in 1956, Rattigan spent two and a half hours informing his Oxford contemporary George Devine why the new play he had discovered would not work in the theatre. When Devine persisted, Rattigan answered 'Then I know nothing about plays.' To which Devine replied, 'You know everything about plays, but you don't know a fucking thing about *Look Back in Anger.*[30] Rattigan only barely attended the first night. He and Hugh Beaumont wanted to leave at the interval until the critic T. C. Worsley persuaded them to stay.[31]

The support for the English Stage Company's initiative was soon overwhelming. Osborne's play was acclaimed by the influential critics Kenneth Tynan and Harold Hobson, and the production was revived frequently at the Court, soon standing as the banner under which that disparate band of men (and women), the Angry Young Men, would assemble. Like many of his contemporaries, Rattigan decried the new movements, Beckett and Ionesco's turn from Naturalism, the wild invective of Osborne, the passionate socialism of Wesker, the increasing influence of Brecht. His opposition to them was perhaps intemperate, but he knew what was at stake: 'I may be prejudiced, but I'm pretty sure it won't survive,' he said in 1960, 'I'm prejudiced because if it *does* survive, I know I won't.'[32]

Such was the power and influence of the new movement that Rattigan almost immediately seemed old-fashioned. And from now on, his plays began to receive an almost automatic panning. His first play since *Separate Tables* (1954) was *Variation on a Theme* (1958). But between those dates the critical mood had changed. To make matters worse, there was the widely publicised story that nineteen-year-old Shelagh Delaney had written the successful *A Taste of Honey* in two weeks after having seen *Variation on a Theme* and deciding that she could do better. A more sinister aspect of the response was the increasingly open accusation that Rattigan was dishonestly concealing a covert homosexual play within an apparently heterosexual one. The two champions of Osborne's play, Tynan and Hobson, were joined by Gerard Fay in the *Manchester Guardian* and Alan Brien in the *Spectator* to ask 'Are Things What They Seem?'[33]

When he is not being attacked for smuggling furtively homosexual themes into apparently straight plays, Rattigan is also criticised for lacking the courage to 'come clean' about his sexuality, both in his life and in his writing.[34] But neither of these criticisms really hit the mark. On the one hand, it is rather disingenuous to suggest that Rattigan should have 'come out'. The 1950s were a difficult time for homosexual men. The flight to the Soviet Union of Burgess and Maclean in 1951 sparked off a major witch-hunt against homosexuals, especially those in prominent positions. Cecil Beaton and Benjamin Britten were rumoured to be targets.[35] The police greatly stepped up the investigation and entrapment of homosexuals and prosecutions rose dramatically at the end of the forties, reaching a peak in 1953–4. One of their most infamous arrests for importuning, in October 1953, was that of John Gielgud.[36]

But neither is it quite correct to imply that somehow Rattigan's plays are *really* homosexual. This would be to misunderstand the way that homosexuality figured in the forties and early fifties. Wartime London saw a considerable expansion in the number of pubs and bars where homosexual men (and women) could meet. This network sustained a highly sophisticated system of gestural and dress codes, words and phrases that could be used to indicate one's sexual desires, many of them drawn from theatrical slang. But the illegality of any homosexual activity ensured that these codes could never become *too* explicit, *too* clear. Homosexuality, then, was explored and experienced through a series of semi-hidden, semi-open codes of behaviour; the image of the iceberg, with the greater part of its bulk submerged beneath the surface, was frequently employed.[37] And this image is, of course, one of the metaphors often used to describe Rattigan's own playwriting.

Reaction came in the form of a widespread paranoia about the apparent increase in homosexuality. The fifties saw a major drive to seek out, understand, and often 'cure' homosexuality. The impetus of these investigations was to bring the unspeakable and underground activities of, famously, 'Evil Men' into the open, to make it fully visible. The Wolfenden Report of 1957 was, without doubt, a certain kind of liberalising document in its recommendation that consensual sex between adult men in private be legalised. However the other side of its effect is to reinstate the integrity of those boundaries – private/public, hidden/exposed, homosexual/heterosexual – which homosexuality was broaching. The criticisms of Rattigan are precisely part of this same desire to divide, clarify and expose.

Many of Rattigan's plays were originally written with explicit homosexual characters (*French Without Tears*, *The Deep Blue*

Sea and *Separate Tables*, for example), which he then changed.[38] But many more of them hint at homosexual experiences and activities: the relationship between Tony and David in *First Episode*, the Major in *Follow My Leader* who is blackmailed over an incident in Baghdad ('After all,' he explains, 'a chap's only human, and it was a deuced hot night – '),[39] the suspiciously polymorphous servicemen of *While the Sun Shines*, Alexander the Great and T. E. Lawrence from *Adventure Story* and *Ross*, Mr Miller in *The Deep Blue Sea* and several others. Furthermore, rumours of Rattigan's own bachelor life circulated fairly widely. As indicated above, Rattigan always placed great trust in the audiences of his plays, and it was the audience that had to decode and reinterpret these plays. His plays cannot be judged by the criterion of 'honesty' and 'explicitness' that obsessed a generation after Osborne. They are plays which negotiate sexual desire through structures of hint, implications and metaphor. As David Rudkin has suggested, 'the craftsmanship of which we hear so much loose talk seems to me to arise from deep psychological necessity, a drive to organise the energy that arises out of his own pain. Not to batten it down but to invest it with some expressive clarity that speaks immediately to people, yet keeps itself hidden.'[40]

The shifts in the dominant view of both homosexuality and the theatre that took place in the fifties account for the brutal decline of Rattigan's career. He continued writing, and while *Ross* (1960) was reasonably well received, his ill-judged musical adaptation of *French Without Tears*, *Joie de Vivre* (1960), was a complete disaster, not assisted by a liberal bout of laryngitis among the cast, and the unexpected insanity of the pianist.[41] It ran for four performances.

During the sixties, Rattigan was himself dogged with ill-health: pneumonia and hepatitis were followed by leukaemia. When his death conspicuously failed to transpire, this last diagnosis was admitted to be incorrect. Despite this, he continued to write, producing the successful television play *Heart to Heart* in 1962, and the stage play *Man and Boy* the following year, which received the same sniping that greeted *Variation on a Theme*. In 1964, he wrote *Nelson – a Portrait in Miniature* for Associated Television, as part of a short season of his plays.

It was at this point that Rattigan decided to leave Britain and live abroad. Partly this decision was taken for reasons of health; but partly Rattigan just seemed no longer to be welcome. Ironically, it was the same charge being levelled at Rattigan that he had faced in the thirties, when the newspapers thundered against the those who had supported the Oxford Union's pacifist motion as 'woolly-minded Communists, practical jokers and sexual indeterminates'.[42] As he confessed in an interview late in his life, 'Overnight almost, we were told we were old-fashioned and effete and corrupt and finished, and... I somehow accepted Tynan's verdict and went off to Hollywood to write film scripts.'[43] In 1967 he moved to Bermuda as a tax exile. A stage adaptation of his Nelson play, as *Bequest to the Nation*, had a lukewarm reception.

Rattigan had a bad sixties, but his seventies seemed to indicate a turnaround in his fortunes and reputation. At the end of 1970, a successful production of *The Winslow Boy* was the first of ten years of acclaimed revivals. In 1972, Hampstead Theatre revived *While the Sun Shines*, and a year later the Young Vic was praised for its *French Without Tears*. In 1976 and 1977 *The Browning Version* was revived at the King's Head and *Separate Tables* at the Apollo. Rattigan briefly returned to Britain in 1971, pulled partly by his renewed fortune and partly by the fact that he was given a knighthood in the New Year's honours list. Another double-bill followed in 1973: *In Praise of Love* comprised the weak *Before Dawn* and the moving tale of emotional concealment and creativity, *After Lydia*. Critical reception was more respectful than usual, although the throwaway farce of the first play detracted from the quality of the second.

Cause Célèbre, commissioned by BBC Radio and others, concerned the Rattenbury case, in which Alma Rattenbury's aged husband was beaten to death by her eighteen-year-old lover. Shortly after its radio premiere, Rattigan was diagnosed with bone cancer. Rattigan's response, having been through the false leukaemia scare in the early sixties, was to greet the news with unruffled elegance, welcoming the opportunity to 'work harder and indulge myself more'.[44] The hard work included a play about the Asquith family and a stage adaptation of *Cause Célèbre*, but, as production difficulties began to arise over the latter, the Asquith play slipped out of Rattigan's grasp. Although very ill, he returned to Britain, and on 4 July 1977, he was taken by limousine from his hospital bed to Her Majesty's Theatre, where he watched his last ever premiere. A fortnight later he had a car drive him around the West End where two of his plays were then running before boarding the plane for the last time. On 30 November 1977, in Bermuda, he died.

As Michael Billington's perceptive obituary noted, 'his whole work is a sustained assault on English middle-class values: fear of emotional commitment, terror in the face of passion, apprehension about sex'.[45] In death, Rattigan began once again to be seen as someone critically opposed to the values with which he had so long been associated, a writer dramatising dark moments of bleak compassion and aching desire.

Notes

1. Quoted in Rattigan's *Daily Telegraph* obituary (1 December 1977).

2. Michael Darlow and Gillian Hodson. *Terence Rattigan: The Man and His Work*. London and New York: Quartet Books, 1979, p. 26.

3. See, for example, Sheridan Morley. 'Terence Rattigan at 65.' *The Times*. (9 May 1977).

4. Terence Rattigan. Preface. *The Collected Plays of Terence Rattigan: Volume Two*. London: Hamish Hamilton, 1953, p. xv.

5. *Ibid.,* p. viii.

6. *Ibid.,* p. vii.

7. *Ibid.,* p. vii.

8. cf. Sheridan Morley, *op. cit.*

9. Humphrey Carpenter. *OUDS: A Centenary History of the Oxford University Dramatic Society*. With a Prologue by Robert Robinson. Oxford: Oxford University Press, 1985, p. 123.

10. Rattigan may well have reprised this later in life. John Osborne, in his autobiography, recalls a friend showing him a picture of Rattigan performing in an RAF drag show: 'He showed me a photograph of himself with Rattigan, dressed in a *tutu*, carrying a wand, accompanied by a line of aircraftsmen, during which Terry had sung his own show-stopper, 'I'm just about the oldest fairy in the business. I'm quite the oldest fairy that you've ever seen".' John Osborne. *A Better Class of Person: An Autobiography, Volume I 1929–1956*. London: Faber and Faber, 1981, p. 223.

11. Darlow and Hodson *op. cit.*, p. 83.

12. Norman Gwatkin. Letter to Gilbert Miller, 28 July 1938. in: *Follow My Leader*. Lord Chamberlain's Correspondence: LR 1938. [British Library].

13. Richard Huggett. *Binkie Beaumont: Eminence Grise of the West Theatre 1933–1973*. London: Hodder & Stoughton, 1989, p. 308.

14. Terence Rattigan. Preface. *The Collected Plays of Terence Rattigan: Volume One*. London: Hamish Hamilton, 1953, p. xiv.

15. George Bernard Shaw, in: Keith Newman. *Two Hundred and Fifty Times I Saw a Play: or, Authors, Actors and Audiences*. With the facsimile of a comment by Bernard Shaw. Oxford: Pelagos Press, 1944, p. 2.

16. Henry Channon. *Chips: The Diaries of Sir Henry Channon*. Edited by Robert Rhodes James. Harmondsworth: Penguin, 1974, p. 480. Entry for 29 September 1944.

17. Tom Driberg. *Ruling Passions*. London: Jonathan Cape, 1977, p. 186.

18. See, for example, Norman Hart. 'Introducing Terence Rattigan,' *Theatre World*. xxxi, 171. (April 1939). p. 180 or Ruth Jordan. 'Another Adventure Story,' *Woman's Journal*. (August 1949), pp. 31–32.

19. Audrey Williamson. *Theatre of Two Decades*. New York and London: Macmillan, 1951, p. 100.

20. Terence Rattigan. 'Concerning the Play of Ideas,' *New Statesman and Nation*. (4 March 1950), pp. 241–242.

21 Terence Rattigan. 'The Play of Ideas,' *New Statesman and Nation*. (13 May 1950), pp. 545–546. See also Susan Rusinko, 'Rattigan versus Shaw: The 'Drama of Ideas' Debate'. in: *Shaw: The Annual of Bernard Shaw Studies: Volume Two*. Edited by Stanley Weintraub. University Park, Penn: Pennsylvania State University Press, 1982. pp. 171–78.

22. John Elsom writes that Rattigan's plays 'represented establishment writing'. *Post-War British Drama*. Revised Edition. London: Routledge, 1979, p. 33.

23. B. A. Young. *The Rattigan Version: Sir Terence Rattigan and the Theatre of Character*. Hamish Hamilton: London, 1986, pp. 102–103; and Darlow and Hodson, *op. cit.*, p. 196, 204n.

24. Terence Rattigan. *Coll. Plays: Vol. Two. op. cit.*, pp. xi–xii.

25. *Ibid.*, p. xii.

26. *Ibid.*, p. xiv.

27. *Ibid.*, p. xvi.

28. *Ibid.*, p. xviii.

29. Opened on 17 September 1960. cf. *Plays and Players*. vii, 11 (November 1960).

30. Quoted in Irving Wardle. *The Theatres of George Devine*. London: Jonathan Cape, 1978, p. 180.

31. John Osborne. *Almost a Gentleman: An Autobiography, Volume II 1955–1966*. London: Faber and Faber, 1991, p. 20.

32. Robert Muller. 'Soul-Searching with Terence Rattigan.' *Daily Mail*. (30 April 1960).

33. The headline of Hobson's review in the *Sunday Times*, 11 May 1958.

34. See, for example, Nicholas de Jongh. *Not in Front of the Audience: Homosexuality on Stage*. London: Routledge, 1992, pp. 55–58.

35. Kathleen Tynan. *The Life of Kenneth Tynan*. Corrected Edition. London: Methuen, 1988, p. 118.

36. Cf. Jeffrey Weeks. *Coming Out: Homosexual Politics in Britain from the Nineteenth Century to the Present*. Revised and Updated Edition. London and New York: Quartet, 1990, p. 58; Peter Wildeblood. *Against the Law*. London: Weidenfeld and Nicolson, 1955, p. 46. The story of Gielgud's arrest may be found in Huggett, *op. cit.*, pp. 429–431. It was Gielgud's arrest which apparently inspired Rattigan to write the second part of *Separate Tables*, although again, thanks this time to the Lord Chamberlain, Rattigan had to change the Major's offence to a heterosexual one. See Darlow and Hodson, *op. cit.*, p. 228.

37. See, for example, Rodney Garland's novel about homosexual life in London, *The Heart in Exile*. London: W. H. Allen, 1953, p. 104.

38. See note 36; and also 'Rattigan Talks to John Simon,' *Theatre Arts*. 46 (April 1962), p. 24.

39. Terence Rattigan and Anthony Maurice. *Follow My Leader*. Typescript. Lord Chamberlain Play Collection: 1940/2. Box 2506. [British Library].

40. Quoted in Darlow and Hodson, *op. cit.*, p. 15.

41. B. A. Young, *op. cit.*, p. 162.

42. Quoted in Darlow and Hodson, *op. cit.*, p. 56.

43. Quoted in Sheridan Morley, *op. cit.*

44. Darlow and Hodson, *op. cit.*, p. 308.

45. *Guardian*. (2 December 1977).

First Episode

On 12 February 1934, a letter arrived at the office of the Lord
Chamberlain, British theatre's official censor, from the Public
Morality Council, a group of self-appointed moral guardians
with a mission to root out vice and blasphemy in culture and
public life. This letter contained a substantial report on a play
that had recently opened at the Comedy Theatre, London: *First
Episode*. Four members of the Council had been to see the play
and found it an 'unpleasant and immoral play, the authors of
which appear to be completely sex-obsessed'. It condemned the
play's 'filthy language', numerous instances of blasphemy, and
one particular 'bedroom scene' that they considered 'revolting
in the extreme'. One of the reporters for the Council judged that
the play 'could do with complete annihilation'.[1]

First Episode was written by Terence Rattigan and Philip
Heimann, and marks Rattigan's professional debut as a
playwright. Given that only twenty-five years later, Rattigan
would be widely dismissed as a writer who pandered to the
more conservative impulses of his audience, it may be
surprising to find him, at the beginning of his career, giving rise
to such moral and sexual outrage. It wasn't only the Public
Morality Council, either. One reviewer remarked: 'I cannot
commend the morals of the piece, which shows a number of
undergraduates a little too preoccupied with sex.'[2]

The university in which the play is set is not named, though most
critics recognised it to be Oxford, even if they found it incredible
that Oxford undergraduates were capable of such debauchery: 'I
refuse to believe,' wrote one, 'that the average Oxford man [...]
is so lacking in decency and moral sense and so ready to yield to
the temptations of drink, gambling and dissipated modes of life
as this play would have us believe.'[3] The disguise was clearly
insufficient for Felix Felton, the president of the Oxford
University Dramatic Society [OUDS] and a successful future
actor, who complained, 'I know that some of the events in the

play have really happened, but when you put them all into one single play the lurid impression you get of what goes on is entirely false. You would think that these violent exceptions were the rule.'[4] Paul Dehn, editor of the Oxford University students' newspaper, *The Cherwell,* and a man who would, thirty years later, collaborate with Rattigan on *Joie de Vivre*, was summoned before the Proctors, the senior officers of the university, 'who told him that they had received letters of protest about *First Episode* from all over the country and issued an edict forbidding him to review the play in his columns'.[5]

Rattigan drew his plays from a variety of sources; sometimes, as in *French Without Tears*, directly from his own life; sometimes, as in *The Deep Blue Sea* and *In Praise of Love*, from the lives of his friends; occasionally from historical events, as in *Ross* and *Cause Célèbre*; and ever so often, as in *After the Dance*, purely from his own imagination. *First Episode* is very clearly in the first category, drawing together and fictionalising a number of different personal experiences at Oxford to make the substance of his play. But it is more than that, too. There are unmistakeable signs in *First Episode* of the mature playwright Rattigan would become, and the play offers fascinating evidence of the sexual and political faultlines that ran through Britain in the 1930s in general, and Rattigan's life and work in particular.

Rattigan began reading History at Trinity College, Oxford, in October 1930. Although he was an intelligent and thoughtful young man, academic studies were not the focus of his attention. Instead, he gravitated towards OUDS and made a series of friendships that would continue to sustain him throughout the rest of his theatre career. It was also at Oxford, away from parental authority, that he began, unapologetically, to express his homosexuality. The fashion designer Bunny Roger recalled that, the first time he met Rattigan at Oxford, 'he was in bed with a rather handsome young man. And did not seem in the least embarrassed.'[6]

One of his closest friends was Philip Heimann, a tall, fair-haired South African student studying Law. The two friends took rooms together in Canterbury House, King Edward Street, along with Peter Glenville, who would go on to direct the premieres of *The*

Winslow Boy and *The Browning Version*. 'Canters', as it was known, was a fashionable address, perfectly suited for lavish parties with its Club Room and central location. Rattigan made no secret that he had sexual feelings for Heimann, but it didn't damage their friendship that these feelings were not reciprocated. Heimann, in fact, was in a relationship with a young woman, Valeria Basilewitch, known as Va-Va. This situation was complicated by the arrival of Va-Va's older sister, Irina, fresh from a divorce, and exuding maturity and sexuality: 'She smoked and painted her nails and was wonderfully *infra dig*.'[7] Heimann soon gave up Va-Va for the irresistible Irina, watched over by the amused – and just a little envious – Rattigan, who soon realised that there was, in the complicated relationship between him, Philip and Irina, the makings of a play.[8]

During Rattigan's second year at Oxford, the presidency of OUDS was taken by George Devine. Almost a quarter of a century later, Devine would found the English Stage Company at the Royal Court, a company that came to symbolise everything that Rattigan was not, but at Oxford they were, if not friends, supportive acquaintances; Devine read an experimental play of Rattigan's and responded encouragingly to it. The main event of Devine's presidency was the OUDS production of *Romeo and Juliet*, for which he invited John Gielgud to direct and Peggy Ashcroft to star as Juliet.[9] Gielgud agreed, bringing with him Edith Evans to play the Nurse and the design team Motley. From the undergraduate body, he cast Devine as Mercutio, Christopher Hassall as Romeo, Hugh Hunt as Friar Lawrence, and William Devlin as Tybalt. Also visible on the stage was Rattigan as the First Musician, whose one line – 'Faith, we may put up our pipes and be gone' – he seemed unable to deliver without convulsing the audience. Each time this happened, he got more and more nervous and more and more unintentionally amusing (an episode which he would incorporate into *Harlequinade*).

There was an undoubted frisson in the production's glamorous mingling of undergraduates and star actors – and an aura of playfulness, boundaries being broken, of flirtatious socialising and youthful high-spiritedness. 'Awed though the boys were by Gielgud, Edith Evans and Peggy Ashcroft,' writes Michael

Darlow, 'there was great competition for their attention. They inundated them with invitations to parties, dinners, and tête-à-têtes,' a description that precisely describes the giddy atmosphere of *First Episode*.[10]

Peggy Ashcroft probably had a particular impact on the play that Rattigan was planning. Michael Billington writes, 'For Peggy it was a happy time both personally and professionally. There was the fun of Oxford itself in the spring term and the chance of mingling with the students: one OUDS member who vividly remembers meeting her at "one of those classic Oxford parties where we all stayed up till six in the morning" was her future third husband, Jeremy Hutchinson.'[11] That marriage was later, but at Oxford she enjoyed the parties, the flirtations, and was rumoured to have had a brief affair with George Devine. Margaret Harris of Motley recalled, 'She was always to some extent in love with somebody [...] Peggy was promiscuous, but it was always with an open spirit. She always loved the people.'[12] This glamorous and flirtatious actress, with her open heart and strong desires, had a decisive effect on Rattigan's characterisation of Margot Gresham.

But at this stage, the play was only an idea, and it was interrupted by Rattigan's renewed attention to his studies. His father, Frank Rattigan, was still determined that Terry would follow him into the Diplomatic Service; he had sent his son to a French crammer in the first two summer breaks while at Oxford – which didn't improve his French but did provide the source material for *French Without Tears*. In his final year, Rattigan studied hard, taking subjects from classical political theory to the emergence of the modern state. The play was not dead; it emerged slowly, in long discussions between Rattigan and Heimann, talking through its plot, characters and ideas, walking together over Christ Church Meadow.

Rattigan's resolve was temporary. His grandmother, Lady Rattigan, died and left him a legacy of £1000 in her will.[13] This sudden access of independent means encouraged Rattigan to try his hand as a theatrical producer. He and Heimann advertised for new plays in the *Morning Post* but were unimpressed both with the plays and the playwrights that responded. Instead, they accelerated the process of writing their own play. And towards the end of his final term, in calculated defiance of his father, Rattigan decided not to sit his exams and so failed to graduate. He kept this back from his father, having already agreed to brush up his German at another crammer in Marzell, near Baden-Baden. He invited Heimann to come with him and, while watching in horrified fascination the early months of the Third Reich, together they finished their play, at this stage titled *Embryo*, which Rattigan parcelled up and sent to a producer in Britain with a track record for new work. Heimann returned to South Africa, and Rattigan returned to the serious business of trying not to learn German.

He was surprised when, only a few weeks later, he received a reply from the producer commending the play and suggesting the Q Theatre in Kew, Surrey. Billing itself as 'A Bright, Cosy Theatre for the Presentation of Successful WEST END PLAYS', the Q Theatre had been a beer garden, a roller-rink and a film studio until Jack and Beatie de Leon converted it into a theatre, seating an audience of four hundred and ninety, devoted, on the model of the Everyman Theatre, Hampstead, to new writing with the potential of transferring to Shaftesbury Avenue. In the thirty years before it closed in the 1950s, they produced hundreds of new plays, many of which ended up in the West End, including one of the great farces of the mid-century, Philip King's *See How They Run* (1944). In addition, they can lay claim to have discovered two major British playwrights: William Douglas-Home, whose *Great Possessions* they produced in 1937, and Terence Rattigan. Rattigan redrafted and retitled the play *Episode* before finally deciding on *First Episode* shortly before its opening night at the Q Theatre on 11 September 1933. Jack de Leon remembered 'almost a good play' with dialogue that was 'easy to speak and with a real sense of character and comedy'.[14]

The play ran for a week and got at least one very favourable review: 'An extremely able and amusing "first play", all unheralded and unchampioned, popped up at the Kew Theatre last week. It is the work of two undergraduates. It gives us an Oxford – or "a certain side of Oxford", as we can reassure ourselves – riddled with betting on horses, not averse to alcohol, and interested, to the point of mania, in young ladies. Nevertheless it

has the ring of being an authentic side.' The reviewer also noted
the skill with which 'the authors have switched the play over in its
last act from being merely a play of juvenile high spirits into a
play in which the characters are real enough to feel pain', finally
adding, 'It is claiming no prophetic gifts to suggest that the play
will probably be seen later in town.'[15]

This prophecy was correct. *First Episode* fitted 1933's taste for
slightly titillating, risqué plays. Avery Hopwood's *Ladies' Night*
(Aldwych Theatre, November 1933) was an extended comedy
sketch set in a Turkish Bath, in which a series of improbable
plot devices force men to dress as women – and women to
undress as women – for the enjoyment of an undemanding
audience. *While Parents Sleep* by Anthony Kimmins (Royalty
Theatre, January 1932, and still running in December 1933) was
a farce in which two brothers bring home two women from
either ends of the social spectrum, Lady Cattering and Miss
'Bubbles' Thompson. While the title seems to announce a
warning about negligent parenting, the plot seemed designed
mainly to offer the frisson of promiscuity and, if *Play Pictorial*
is to be trusted, the teasing display of stockings and
suspenders.[16] More serious perhaps were *The Wind and the Rain*
by Merton Hodge (St Martin's, October 1933) and *The Old
Folks at Home* by H.M. Harwood (Queen's Theatre, December
1933), both of which depicted young people as a slang-talking,
sexually promiscuous, drinking and drug-taking breed. *The
Wind and the Rain*, in particular, was set among undergraduates
and no doubt encouraged the producer, Daniel Mayer, to a West
End transfer for *First Episode*. With a cast strengthened by the
introduction of William Fox as Tony and Barbara Hoffe as
Margot, *First Episode* opened at the Comedy Theatre on 26
January 1934, in a production by the silkily named Muriel Pratt.
The programme notes that the set featured a genuine painting
by the post-impressionist Auguste Herbin, lent by the Mayor
Gallery on Cork Street. It also discloses, reassuringly, that 'this
theatre is disinfected throughout by Jeyes'.

Friends from Oxford mingled in the disinfected stalls with the
national critics. Philip Heimann flew back from Johannesburg
for his West End debut. The play was enormously well-
received, with full-throated laughter greeting its first

two-and-a-half acts, and hushed silence its final scene. Max
Adrian was particularly admired for his performance as Bertie
and Patrick Waddington's comic turn at the beginning of the
third act was hugely applauded, particularly for a moment
where, mid-sentence, he slid drunkenly from the bed and,
oblivious, delivered the rest of his speech with his feet in the air
and his head on the floor. Rattigan and Heimann took to the
stage for the curtain call, wearing contrasting red and white
carnations, to wild cheers.

When the two recovered sufficiently from their first-night party
to read their press, they were amazed to discover themselves
widely celebrated authors. 'The two youthful authors of this
brilliant first play about life as it is not usually lived at Oxford
University have done better than back a winner; I believe they
have written one,' announced the *Sunday Referee*.[17] 'Granted
that somehow no play about university life is entirely
acceptable,' noted the *Evening News*, '*First Episode* at the
Comedy Theatre, seems to me about as good a specimen as one
can expect'.[18] The *Illustrated London News* warned that 'many
playgoers will regard this as decidedly vulgar. And they will be
right,' but added, 'it is also extremely amusing.'[19]

Some critics were confused by the play's move from light
comedy to serious drama. *The Times* found the comedy more
successful than the drama, and the *Saturday Review* regretted
that the play ended on a 'sad note'. The *Independent* felt that
the play should have been more, not less, serious. James Agate
in the *Sunday Times* thought the play notable for 'the avenues
which it declines to explore'.[20] In fact, the play's shape – its
balance between comedy and drama, its expression of serious,
complex ideas within a sex comedy – was the product of a long
process, and, in some ways, the West End production hid rather
than revealed the play's sophistication.

Rattigan generously gave a co-writing credit to his friend Philip
Heimann, but it is unlikely that Heimann did much of the actual
writing. It is true that the story was loosely based on Heimann's
romantic entanglements and that the two young men planned
the play out in long discussions at Oxford. But the language
feels like early Rattigan, and, indeed, Heimann's name was only
added to the title page of the manuscript at a late stage.[21]

Heimann, too, was in South Africa from summer 1933 to late January 1934, and can have played little role in the extensive redrafting that took place during the Q Theatre and Comedy Theatre rehearsals and between the two productions.

Successive drafts of *First Episode* enable us to trace the emergence of the play from the early version submitted for production at the Q Theatre to the extensive revisions prepared for the West End opening. The earliest draft that has survived is the one sent to the Lord Chamberlain for approval before production at the Q Theatre. The censor did not have a high opinion of the play: 'This is terrible trash; plot, characterisation, construction, and dialogue all crudely amateurish,' he pronounced, rather unfairly. More seriously, he was concerned by three areas of the play's 'crudely sophisticated dialogue'.[22] The first is blasphemy: the Lord Chamberlain informs the theatre management that 'the word "God" occurs too frequently, and I am to request that you will indicate which of these will be deleted'.[23] The second area concerned explicit and unapologetic references to casual sex. Two passages of dialogue between David and Margot were marked for deletion:

MARGOT. She's probably very much in love with you and you admit yourself you've only got one use for her.

DAVID. So you think I use her just to satisfy my own selfish pleasure, do you?

MARGOT. Well, you take what she gives you and you don't give her anything in return.

DAVID. So in your opinion she's making a great sacrifice in granting me favours?

MARGOT. I don't say that, exactly, but at least she expects some return for it.

DAVID. You talk about her as if she were a prostitute. Don't you think she gets any pleasure out of it herself?

This dialogue makes it explicit not only that David and Joan have slept together but, perhaps even more scandalously, that Joan has enjoyed it. A later (also forbidden) passage has David remark that 'I like sleeping with her and because, though you may not believe it, she adores sleeping with me. That's the only thing we have in common. I don't believe she really wants me in any other way, and if she imagines she does it's only to satisfy her vanity,' which goes further in suggesting that sex might be an end in itself, not necessarily part of a loving or marital relationship.[24]

The third area to which the Lord Chamberlain pays particular attention is any suggestion of homosexuality. The play never makes any direct declaration that David and Tony's relationship or David's feelings for Tony might be sexual, though it is hinted at throughout and is an idea that preoccupies Margot; in the earliest draft, Tony tells David: 'She seems to think you're trying to take me away from her. Once she lost her temper and accused us of being a couple of pansies.'[25] The examiner recommends that this reference be deleted, though he allows the – slightly vaguer – accusation 'filthy degenerate' to stand.

The Lord Chamberlain was not censoring these ideas about sex and sexuality because they were in some way unthinkable; they were extremely thinkable and were being widely thought. The 1920s had seen a loosening of attitudes towards sexuality; the 'bright young things' promoted an image of promiscuity and pleasure, while groups of bohemians experimented with new attitudes and ways of living.[26] Bertrand Russell's best-selling *Marriage and Morals* (1929) defended sex before and outside marriage, and Ben B. Lindsey's influential *The Companionate Marriage*, which argued that marriages should have a trial period and divorce be simply arranged by mutual consent, was published in Britain in 1928. Even in more mainstream publications, these ideas were beginning to be openly expressed. Jeffrey Weeks recalls that 'The *Lady's Companion* had drawn attention to a new interest in sex as early as 1920, while *Good Housekeeping* had noted the importance of Freud in convincing women that they had sex drives.'[27] Sexologists and campaigners like Havelock Ellis, Marie Stopes, Theodoor Hendrik van de Velde encouraged the still-new idea that sex was a pleasurable activity for both men and women.

The public profile of homosexuality was changing in the 1920s. Weeks notes that in 1920, homosexual offences were considered so indecent that they could not be mentioned in a newspaper.[28]

However, part of the decade's bohemianism was a growing confidence among the 'queer' underground. Halfway through the decade, *John Bull* magazine felt it necessary to denounce the number of establishments ('bogus hotels... assignation houses... undesirable dens... mere haunts of evil,' it frothed) in which gay men were able to meet.[29] *First Episode* opened at the Comedy Theatre around the same time as The Caravan Club, ten minutes' walk away on Endell Street. An advertising flyer of the time described it as 'London's Greatest Bohemian Rendezvous said to be the most unconventional spot in town' and promising 'All-Night Gaiety'. Theatres themselves were sites in which homosexual men, in particular, could meet in relative openness. The Circle Bar of the Palladium Theatre, for example, was a well-known place for homosexual men to make assignations.[30] One man, recalling the mid-1920s, remembers managing to have sex with another man in the rear gallery of the Prince of Wales Theatre, during a performance of Arnold Ridley's *The Ghost Train*.[31]

Campaigners called for a clampdown on these activities and a return to traditional family values, and found a sympathetic ear in the notoriously puritanical and anti-semitic Sir William Joynson-Hicks, who was Home Secretary between 1924 and 1929.[32] Among other things, he pursued a vindictive prosecution of Radclyffe Hall's lesbian novel, *The Well of Loneliness* (1928), taking his cue from an inflammatory editorial in the *Sunday Express* which declared, 'I would rather give a healthy boy or a healthy girl a phial of prussic acid than this novel. Poison kills the body, but moral poison kills the soul,' and demanded, 'This book must at once be withdrawn.'[33] The prosecution was mirrored in a new police crackdown on acts of 'gross indecency' between men: in London, arrests for importuning rose from ten in 1929 to one hundred and thirteen in 1930 and seventy-eight in 1931.[34]

The Lord Chamberlain's function as state censor of plays made him a key figure in this campaign for moral purity, and his judgements are very often plainly ideological. It's striking that he bans the reference to 'pansies' and yet notes of the word 'bitch' that 'this is a natural remark and I should leave it in'.[35] However, the Lord Chamberlain was not a wholly conservative

figure, and the examiners often prided themselves on their
theatrical sophistication. They were caught between the
morality campaigners on one side and the theatre-makers on the
other, and they seem to have tried hard to satisfy both camps.

First Episode provides a good example of the complexity of the
situation. When the Public Morality Council submit their report
on the play, the Lord Chamberlain sends an examiner to visit
the play and invites the General Secretary to come in to discuss
his organisation's concerns in person. Since 1926, the Public
Morality Council had been granted this kind of special access –
not something accorded to many institutions – and they made
frequent use of this privilege. In this instance, the letter from
Howard Tyrer implies that he is unconvinced of the show's
venality but is acting on the wishes of the Plays Committee and
so encloses the reports of '1. Miss Neville, 2. Miss Plume, 3.
Mrs Davidson, 4. Our Chief Inspector'. (That is should take
four people to determine whether a play is immoral is curious
and reminds one of Jeffrey Weeks's comments on the Council's
endless reporting of indecent acts taking place in public parks,
'which conveys an irresistible picture of respectable ladies
pursuing their moral passion to the point of prying'.[36])

The four reports offer clear evidence of the sexual anxieties of
the time. Two of the reporters offer detailed accounts of the
'bedroom scene' (Act Three, Scene One): 'Joan, very drunk, is
going to bed. She undresses and gets into bed and David enters
equally and disgustingly drunk. He lies on the bed beside her
outside the bedclothes. They roll about drunkenly together and
David sits on the floor with the slop pail beside him.' Even
though they are not even touching – one is above the bedsheets,
the other below – it is the physical unrestraint that stands in for
moral disorder in the minds of the reporters. Even more
troubling is that, in the play, this moral disorder is being
perpetrated by 'young men and women, supposedly with the
advantage of a good education'; another reporter writes that 'the
play is supposed to depict the doings of undergraduates and, if
true to life, reflects no credit on any collegian'. There is an
anxiety visible here about the propriety of our great institutions
– echoed in the nervous review of the play published in *The
Sphere* which noted that the bedroom scene 'could not have

happened in pre-war Oxford; but my knowledge of post-war Oxford being almost nil, I would not care the swear that it could not happen today'. There is a clear line being drawn in these responses from physical disorder to moral disorder to social disorder. At stake is moral ownership of British public identity, about which the report is contradictory: 'The public do not want such plays,' insists one report; 'I regret deeply to say that the audience shouted with laughter,' says another.[37]

The Lord Chamberlain's office, while courteous in its official dealings with the Public Morality Council, did not defer to their view. Henry Game visited the play in February and noted that indeed there had been some unauthorised changes of script but found that 'generally speaking the complaints of the P.M.C. seem to me entirely unjustified and probably arise from a confusion in the minds of its members between life at a university and that at a public school and between the functions of the theatre and a Sunday school'.[38] There is no record of the Lord Chamberlain taking any action as a result of the complaint.

Yet the episode makes clear that Rattigan and Heimann had hit a nerve with this play. The story has, in some ways, a very conventional shape: it is a love triangle. Usually, such stories involve two men as rivals for the love of a woman, or perhaps two women competing for the love of a man. In *First Episode*, we see a man and a woman, David and Margot, battling for the love of a man, Tony. David's love for Tony is only obliquely referred to:

> MARGOT. It's a funny friendship between you and Tony. He's a sentimentalist, isn't he?

> DAVID. I didn't think so until tonight.

> MARGOT. The friendship of young men can be very selfish.

> DAVID. But so impregnable. (p. 27)

Later, Margot returns to this 'friendship', determined to test it further:

> DAVID. What is Tony's affair, is mine.

> MARGOT. Why?

DAVID. Because of our friendship.

MARGOT. 'Friendship'?

DAVID. Of course, that is hardly something I could expect you to understand.

MARGOT. I understand it better than you think. I'm not altogether blind.

DAVID. Aren't you?

MARGOT. You think I don't see through all this clever talk.

DAVID. No, I didn't mean that.

MARGOT. Well, I do see through it. (p. 74–75)

These hints, combined with her cruder accusations of depravity (p. 75) and degeneracy (p. 80), imply that Margot is accusing David of homosexual feelings for Tony. Tony notably doesn't refute the charge; he simply throws it back at her: 'You who come down here and seduce a boy half your age [...] you talk about degeneracy.' (p. 80)

What Margot is probing is the continuum between male authority, male friendships and homosexuality: what some have called 'homosociality'. Eve Kosofsky Sedgwick in *Between Men: English Literature and Homosocial Desire* argues that this continuum is complex and contested, and that where the boundary sits between male friendship and male homosexuality is historically variable. She cites Gayle Rubin arguing that 'patriarchal heterosexuality can best be discussed in terms of one or another form of the traffic in women: it is the use of women as exchangeable, perhaps symbolic, property for the primary purpose of cementing the bonds of men with men'.[39] What Rattigan does is to display the mechanisms of these bonds and dares to draw attention to the boundary between homosociality and homosexuality. The play begins with men alone and ends with men alone: the women come and go, traded between the men (Joan passes from Tony to David to Bertie), and in the climactic scene the men unite to expel Margot from the house while their own connection seems deeper than ever (David *'realises all that is passing through* TONY*'s mind, but not a word is said'* (p. 103)). The play draws attention to the ways that male power and male friendship are founded on and maintained by the exclusion of women.

What stops the play from simply reproducing the misogyny of that gesture is the seriousness with which the character of Margot is drawn. In the successive drafts that led to the Comedy Theatre script, she emerges more and more as a rounded, autonomous character. In the first draft, she is rather more two-dimensional: something of a melodramatic villain. As she sees she's losing Tony, she announces, 'There is one part of you that's completely mine, isn't there? If David tries to rob me of that, I won't let him. I'll do anything. (*Desperately.*) I think I'd kill him.'[40] Later, goaded by his comment on her degeneracy, Rattigan has her '*breathless with rage*' and advancing menacingly on David with the words, 'I'll pay you out for this, you swine.'[41] In the first draft, Margot dreams up the idea of informing the Proctors about David's liaison with Joan herself; in the later draft, David puts the idea in her head.

In addition, between the earlier and later drafts, Margot has become a woman of much more independent sexuality. In the Q Theatre draft, she returns to Tony's room innocently believing that they are to rehearse a scene from *Antony and Cleopatra*. By the final draft, her wide-eyed questions about the rehearsal have been replaced by this confident sexual flirtation:

MARGOT. Everyone gone to bed?

TONY. Yes.

MARGOT. How exciting – alone in a man's rooms after midnight. (*Sits on the sofa and puts her legs up*.) (p. 33)

At the end of the scene, in the first draft, Tony takes the initiative in the seduction:

> *He holds her coat and as she slips into it, he loses control, and takes her in his arms and kisses her.*

TONY (*immediately frightened*). I'm sorry, please forgive me.

MARGOT (*rather dazed*). It's all right.

> TONY, *relieved that she is not annoyed, kisses her again, this time more passionately.*

MARGOT *pushes him away.*

MARGOT. Please don't.

TONY. Oh, Margot, I'm sorry. Only you're so lovely...[42]

Tony is sexually active, Margot is the conventional woman defending her honour. In the final draft, she is making the running, and Tony is running to catch up.[43]

The total effect of these rewrites is to make Margot a forerunner of Rattigan characters like Millie Crocker-Harris, Hester Collyer and Alma Rattenbury: intelligent, sexual, strong and independent women. Theatrically, the smartest moment in the play juxtaposes the boorish male undergraduates offstage cheering on their horse, with Margot, alone on stage, suffering the pain of heartbreak (p. 78). Her departure at the end of the play is quietly dignified, rather than triumphantly humiliated. And, scattered through various drafts, there are signs of Rattigan's growing compassion for Margot. In a fragment of dialogue written for the Comedy Theatre but discarded, Margot talks to Joan:

JOAN. You don't look very well, Margot. You're not ill, are you?

MARGOT (*suddenly breaking down*). Oh, Joan, I'm so unhappy.

JOAN. Unhappy? Why, Margot?

MARGOT. I love him so much. You don't understand – it's a terrible thing to love anyone as much as I do. It hurts – oh, it hurts so horribly. (*She is sobbing.*)

JOAN (*going to her and trying to comfort her*). Margot darling –

MARGOT. If only I'd never come to this place at all. Why was I such a fool? I should have known – I should have known –

JOAN. Margot, I hate to see you like this.

MARGOT (*recovering; half to herself*). They're so fiendishly cruel these young men. Perhaps they don't

> realise what it is to be hurt as I've been hurt. Or perhaps
> they do. Perhaps they're like little boys tearing flies to
> pieces just for fun.[44]

The language is a little overheated, but there's no mistaking the
attempt to express Margot's feeling, her pain. By the final draft,
it's cleaner and clearer, and is an unmistakeable sign of the
emotional power Rattigan will bring to his later work.

> JOAN. It's a grand life, I think.

> MARGOT. At your age, I suppose it is. Nothing matters
> much when you're twenty. Somehow I think one's heart
> doesn't beat at twenty, it just lies waiting to get hurt like
> some dumb thing that must suffer without crying out.
> (p. 84)

First Episode is a rehearsal of one of the themes that would
dominate his work: the pain of unequal passion. Indeed, as
Rattigan scholar Susan Rusinko observes, the play is filled with
'issues which consistently reappear in Rattigan's later dramas.
Close male friendships, unequal romances between an older and
a younger person with one feeling deeply the need to give and
the other to receive love, filial conflicts, the growth of boy into
man, the frustrations and pains as innocence gives way to
experience leaving in its wake deep ambivalences – these
profoundly human situations increase and intensify with almost
every play Rattigan wrote.'[45]

What is less easy to see from this distance is how contemporary
the play was. From the Modernist painting on the wall to the
absolutely up-to-the-minute use of slang, the play was
determinedly a play of the 1930s. It is a striking moment when
the undergraduates mockingly parody Noël Coward (p. 67–68):
even though they are often lumped together by theatre
historians, Rattigan and Coward were of different generations
and Rattigan was fiercely conscious of his profound difference
from his older colleague.[46] Rattigan's own political views are
preserved in David, who is President of the Pacifist Club.
Towards the end of Rattigan's third year, he was one of two
hundred and seventy-five students who voted in favour of the
debating motion: 'This House will in no circumstances fight for
King and Country' in the Oxford Union.

His tastes in theatre were, at this point, still uneasily split between Modernist experimentation and the artful storytelling grace of the well-made play. There is an intriguing moment at the end of the Q Theatre version of *First Episode*. After Margot has been expelled from the house, Tony and David mark her departure and then discuss the future:

TONY. Well, what are you going to do, David, when you go down?

DAVID. Oh, I'll go home like the prodigal son, to my people, and after a time they'll forgive me, and then I'll try to earn some money.

TONY. How?

DAVID. Well, I can always write. For that matter, so can you, Tony. We might write something together.

TONY. What, a novel?

DAVID. Yes, if you like. They say there's more money in plays.

TONY. What could we write a play about? We know nothing about life.

DAVID. We don't have to know anything about life. All we need know is about our own lives. What better material could we have? (*Suddenly enthusiastic*.) Look here, Tony, let's do it. We'll write a play about everything that's happened since Margot came.

TONY (*catching his enthusiasm*). Yes, we might. (*Doubtfully*.) Of course, we'd have to cut some of the things out. The public 'ud never stand for them.

DAVID. All right, then, we'll tone it down.

TONY. And we'd have to give it a happy ending, of course. No audience would stand for this drab ending. I'll tell you what we'll do. We'll make Margot go off with you. That 'ud be a clever twist.

DAVID. That's not a bad idea. We'll do that, we'll make Margot go off with me. We can make it seem possible if

we're clever enough. After all, I have admitted she's a
damned attractive woman.

They are lost in thought as –

THE CURTAIN COMES DOWN[47]

It's an intriguing moment of teasing reflexivity that recalls a
contemporary playwright like Pirandello. It does several things; on
one level, it suggests that the events of the play really happened; it
draws attention, in a characteristically High Modernist style, to the
complex status of the text as text; but it also stakes out the play's
dramaturgical territory, because the decisions Tony and David
make are precisely *not* the ones that Terry and Philip made: they
haven't given the play a happy ending; they haven't shied away
from outraging the audience. The original ending lifts us out of the
fictional world to reflect on the nature of playwriting and its
relation to reality. It perhaps strikes an awkward note at the end of
an otherwise dramaturgically conventional play, and it is
unsurprising that Rattigan changed it, but it is a rare glimpse into
his more experimental theatrical inclinations.

Many critics predicted a long run for *First Episode*. Rattigan
certainly enjoyed his new profile as a playwright and rented a
flat in London with Philip Heimann. In April 1934, *Theatre
World* announced that 'Terence has finished another play with
Philip Heimann and has also written one by himself which
Patrick Waddington tells me is brilliantly clever. Keep an eye on
this young man.'[48] This was probably an exaggeration, and in
any case *First Episode* closed on 14 April after eighty-nine
performances. Rattigan had put £200 of his grandmother's
money into the production and – apart from a £100 advance,
split with Philip Heimann – got none of the money back, his
contract having stipulated a very high box-office return before
royalties could be awarded. In the best week of the run, the show
was only making £150, and in mid-February one theatregoer
observed that the audience was bulked out by people holding
free tickets.[49] Heimann decided to marry Irina and move to
South Africa. With no income, Rattigan moved back into his
parents' home. A New York production at the Ritz Theatre with
Max Adrian and David Waddington from the London cast was
met with mixed reviews and closed after forty performances.

First Episode was the play that launched Rattigan's career and gave him a taste of life as a professional playwright. Apart from its brief New York run, it seems to have been revived only once, in October 1938, by the Rex Leslie-Smith Players on Brighton's West Pier, where it was admired 'for the stirring episodes and lambent wit which irradiate it from start to finish'.[50] A West End revival was planned in 1978 in the aftermath of Rattigan's death, for which Philip Heimann was tracked down in South Africa, but the production did not transpire. Rattigan did not publish the play when it was first performed, nor did he include it in his *Collected Plays*; at one point he even claimed, falsely, to have burnt his only copy. Perhaps he felt it was juvenilia; perhaps, as Michael Darlow suggests, the play 'revealed with touching, but to him embarrassing, clarity his own homosexuality and the inner struggle connected with it'.[51] Yet it was the play which launched his professional career, attracted a series of excellent reviews, and achieved a respectable, if unspectacular, West End run. It is a young man's play, dramatically awkward in some ways, but witty, subtle and daring. It was the first episode of his writing career, but not the last.

A Note on the Text

There are six versions of *First Episode* in existence. There are two copies in the Rattigan archive at the British Library; the first seems to coincide with the Q Theatre production and contains multiple manuscript changes and additions; the second seems to be the Comedy Theatre script and also contains multiple manuscript changes. The Lord Chamberlain's collection, also at the British Library, contains the copies of the play submitted for the Q Theatre and Comedy Theatre productions – both of these are substantially different from the corresponding versions in the Rattigan archive. The Comedy Theatre text also contains multiple pasted-in passages of alternative typed dialogue, which do not appear in Rattigan's own copy. There is a version of the play distributed by Rattigan's agent, Michael Imison, in the 1970s. And there is a version held by Rattigan's current agent, Alan Brodie, which appears to have been produced by retyping the second copy in Rattigan's archive, incorporating the manuscript changes on the text, but ignoring those made on the facing pages.

Each of these is different; none of them is clearly definitive. Some of the differences between the scripts are very substantial. In preparing this edition, I have had to establish a definitive text from the drafts available. In doing so, I have attempted to be guided by what I think Rattigan's intentions were. However, he intended different things at different times. Some changes were forced on the play by directors, actors or censors. Some changes appear to be restless tinkering. The status of some changes is impossible to tell (various alterations to manuscripts are not in Rattigan's handwriting). Some of the changes don't make sense of the rest of the play, and should probably be disregarded. This has not been a simple matter.

While following Rattigan's intentions, I have assumed, reasonably enough, that he intended the play to be coherent and also as good as possible. For that reason, I have not always chosen the final version of a particular speech or scene. In the rewrites for the West End production, for example, it seems to me that Rattigan too happily cut some of the more serious material on the request of the director, so I have reinstated it. On the other hand, there is a rather delightful scene of romantic awkwardness between Joan and Bertie (pp. 46–47) that seems not to have been incorporated, and I have retained it. Most of the Lord Chamberlain's deletions are no longer necessary, so I have rescued those passages from deletion; one joke, however, which the censor considered blasphemous is more likely to offend a modern audience by being catastrophically unfunny, so I have let the deletion stand.

Inevitably, this has meant straying beyond pure textual scholarship into artistic judgements; and, inevitably, this edition means that there are now *seven* versions of *First Episode*. I hope you'll find that this new edition is to the benefit of the play and its reputation.

DAN REBELLATO

Notes

1. Letter from Mr H.M. Tyrer [General Secretary of the Public Morality Council] to Major Gordon, Lord Chamberlain's Office, 12 February 1934. Lord Chamberlain's Correspondence: *First Episode*, 1934/12646. British Library.

2. 'Gay Goings On'. An unsigned, unattributed review in a packet of cuttings, in the Production File: *First Episode*, Comedy Theatre, January 1934. V&A Blythe House Archive (henceforth *V&A Production File*).

3. 'A Tragedy of Calf Love'. *Independent*. 10 February 1934, in a scrapbook of reviews kept by Philip Heimann and currently in the possession of his daughter-in-law Diana Heimann (henceforth *Heimann Scrapbook*).

4. 'Is Oxford Like That?' *News Chronicle*. N.D. Production File: *First Episode*, *op. cit.*

5. 'Undergraduate Play: Proctors of Oxford Ban Magazine Review'. *News Chronicle*, 16 February 1934, *Heimann Scrapbook*, *op. cit.*

6. Geoffrey Wansell. *Terence Rattigan: A Biography*. London: Fourth Estate, 1995, p. 50.

7. Diana Heimann. Personal conversation. 27 May 2011.

8. This story has been mangled many times in the retelling. Michael Darlow's otherwise excellent biography (*Terence Rattigan: The Man and His Work*. London: Quartet, 2000) renames Irina 'Irma' and does not mention 'Va-Va'. Geoffrey Wansell's (*op. cit.*) conflates the two sisters. I'm grateful to Diana Heimann for clarifying the history.

9. Until the 1960s, women were not permitted to join OUDS.

10. Darlow, *op. cit.*, pp. 68-69.

11. Michael Billington. *Peggy Ashcroft*. London: John Murray, 1988, p. 49.

12. Garry O'Connor. *The Secret Woman: A Life of Peggy Ashcroft*. London: Weidenfeld and Nicolson, 1997, p. 38.

13. This is equivalent to around £49,000 in 2011.

14. Kenneth Barrow. *On Q: Jack and Beatie De Leon and the Q Theatre*. Richmond: De Leon Memorial Fund, 1992, p. 90.

15. 'H.G.' [Review.] 17 September 1933. Publication unknown. *V&A Production File*.

16. *The Play Pictorial*, Vol 60, No. 361 (April 1932), pp. 56–57. There is a brief clip of the original production on the British Pathé archive website: http://www.britishpathe.com/record.php?id=9011.

17. Review. 28 January 1934. *Heimann Scrapbook*, *op. cit.*

18. J.G.B. 'An Actress Goes to Oxford'. *Evening News*. n.d. *V&A Production File*.

19. 'The Playhouses'. *Illustrated London News*. 3 February 1934, p. 182.

20. *The Times*. 27 January 1934, p. 8; *Saturday Review*. 10 February 1934; *Independent*, 10 February 1934 (both *Heimann Scrapbook*); James Agate. Review. *Sunday Times*. 28 January 1934, quoted in Darlow, *op. cit.*, p. 87.

21. Wansell, *op. cit.*, p. 60.

22. H.C. Game. Report. 16 August 1933. Lord Chamberlain's Correspondence: *Episode*, 1933/12263. British Library.

23. Letter. Lord Chamberlain's Office to Norman Gibson. 21 August 1933. *Ibid.*

24. Terence Rattigan and Philip Heimann. *Episode*. Rattigan Papers: British Library. Add. MSS. 74289, pp. 72–73.

25. *Ibid.*, p. 65.

26. See, for example, D. J. Taylor. *Bright Young Things: The Rise and Fall of a Generation 1918–1940*. London: Chatto & Windus, 2007; and Virginia Nicholson. *Among the Bohemians: Experiments in Living 1900-1939*. Viking: London, 2002.

27. Jeffrey Weeks. *Sex, Politics and Society: The Regulation of Sexuality since 1800*. Second ed. London and New York: Longman, 1989, p. 205.

28. *Ibid.*, p. 200.

29. Matt Houlbrook. *Queer London: Perils and Pleasures in the Sexual Metropolis, 1918–1957*. Chicago: University of Chicago Press, 2005, p. 123.

30. *Ibid.*, pp. 70–71.

31. Kevin Porter and Jeffrey Weeks. *Between the Acts: Lives of Homosexual Men 1885–1967*. London: Routledge, 1991, pp. 74–75.

32. David Cesarani. 'Joynson-Hicks and the Radical Right in England after the First World War.' *Traditions of Intolerance: Historical Perspectives on Fascism and Race Discourse in Britain*. Eds. Tony Kushner and Kenneth Lunn. Manchester: Manchester University Press, 1989. pp. 118–39.

33. Quoted in Richard Dellamora. *Radclyffe Hall: A Life in the Writing*. Philadelphia: University of Pennsylvania Press, 2011, p. 194.

34. Houlbrook, *op. cit.*, p. 32.

35. H.C. Game. Report. 16 August 1933, *op. cit.*

36. Weeks, *op. cit.*, p. 214.

37. All quotations from Letter from Mr H.M. Tyrer to Major Gordon, Lord Chamberlain's Office, 12 February 1934, *op. cit.*

38. H.C. Game. Report. n.d. Lord Chamberlain's Correspondence: *First Episode*, 1934/12646. British Library.

39. Eve Kosofsky Sedgwick. *Between Men: English Literature and Homosocial Desire*. New York: Columbia University Press, 1992, pp. 25–26.

40. Rattigan and Heimann. *Episode*. Rattigan Papers: British Library, *op. cit.*, p. 76.

41. *Ibid.*, p. 101.

42. *Ibid.*, p. 37.

43. Joan and Bertie also benefit enormously from the rewrites. In the earlier drafts they barely know each other, which makes their flirtation simply comic. By the later drafts, they have already been seeing each other which allows their relationship to become richer and funnier (and Bertie's line 'Joan, have you ever lived on a farm?' (p. 65) – which the Lord Chamberlain insisted on censoring – is probably the best joke in the play).

44. Terence Rattigan and Philip Heimann. *First Episode*. Rattigan Papers: British Library. Add. MSS. 74290, inserted as new Act Three pp. 3–4.

45. Susan Rusinko. *Terence Rattigan*. Boston: Twayne, 1983, pp. 33–34.

46. Rattigan wrote a sharply critical article for *The Cherwell* (which he wanted to call 'No, No, Noël') denouncing Coward for the conservative drift of his writing and his embrace of commerce. See Darlow, *op. cit.*, pp. 66–67.

47. Rattigan and Heimann. *Episode*. Rattigan Papers: British Library, *op. cit.*, p. 104–5.

48. Cutting in *V&A Production File*.

49. H.C. Game. Report. n.d., *op. cit.* 'Papering the house' was and is a common practice to get a warmer response in the auditorium and, with luck, generate good word of mouth.

50. Review. *Brighton Standard*, 6 October 1938. Rattigan Papers: British Library. Add. MSS. 74544. The production included a young Jon Pertwee who writes about his time in the company in his autobiography *Moon Boots and Dinner Suits*. London: Elm Tree, 1984.

51. Darlow. *op. cit.*, p. 83.

List of Rattigan's Produced Plays

TITLE	BRITISH PREMIERE	NEW YORK PREMIERE
First Episode (with Philip Heimann)	Q Theatre, Kew, 11 Sept 1933 (transferred to Comedy Theatre, 26 Jan 1934)	Ritz Theatre, 17 Sept 1934
French Without Tears	Criterion Theatre, 6 Nov 1936	Henry Miller Theatre, 28 Sept 1937
After the Dance	St James's Theatre, 21 June 1939	
Follow My Leader (with Anthony Maurice, alias Tony Goldschmidt)	Apollo Theatre, 16 Jan 1940	
Grey Farm (with Hector Bolitho)		Hudson Theatre, 3 May 1940
Flare Path	Apollo Theatre, 13 Aug 1932	Henry Miller Theatre, 23 Dec 1942
While the Sun Shines	Globe Theatre, 24 Dec 1943	Lyceum Theatre, 19 Sept 1944
Love in Idleness	Lyric Theatre, 20 Dec 1944	Empire Theatre (as *O Mistress Mine*), 23 Jan 1946
The Winslow Boy	Lyric Theatre, 23 May 1946	Empire Theatre, 29 Oct 1947
Playbill (*The Browning Version* and *Harlequinade*)	Phoenix Theatre, 8 Sept 1948	Coronet Theatre, 12 Oct 1949
Adventure Story	St James's Theatre, 17 March 1949	
A Tale of Two Cities (from Charles Dickens, with John Gielgud)	St Brendan's College Dramatic Society, Clifton, 23 Jan 1950	
Who is Sylvia?	Criterion Theatre, 24 Oct 1950	

Final Test (TV)	BBC TV, 29 July 1951	
The Deep Blue Sea	Duchess Theatre, 6 Mar 1952	Morosco Theatre, 5 Nov 1952
The Sleeping Prince	Phoenix Theatre, 5 Nov 1953	Coronet Theatre, 1 Nov 1956
Seperate Tables (*The Table by the Window* and *Table Number Seven*)	St James's Theatre, 22 Sept 1954	Music Box Theatre, 25 Oct 1956
Variation on a Theme	Globe Theatre, 8 May 1958	
Ross	Theatre Royal Haymarket 12 May 1960	Eugene O'Neill Theatre 26 Dec 1961
Joie de Vivre (with Robert Stolz and Paul Dehn)	Queen's Theatre, 14 July 1960	
Heart to Heart (TV)	BBC TV, 6 Dec 1962	
Man and Boy	Queen's Theatre, 4 Sept 1963	Brooks Atkinson Theatre, 12 Nov 1963
Ninety Years On (TV)	BBC TV, 29 Nov 1964	
Nelson – A Portrait in Miniature (TV)	Associated Television, 21 Mar 1966	
All On Her Own (TV) (adapted for the stage as *Duologue*)	BBC 2, 25 Sept 1968	
A Bequest to the Nation	Theatre Royal Haymarket 23 Sept 1970	
High Summer (TV)	Thames TV, 12 Sept 1972	
In Praise of Love (*After Lydia* and *Before Dawn*)	Duchess Theatre, 27 Sept 1973	Morosco Theatre, 10 Dec 1974
Cause Célèbre (radio)	BBC Radio 4, 27 Oct 1975	
Duologue	King's Head Theatre, 21 Feb 1976	
Cause Célèbre (stage)	Her Majesty's Theatre, 4 July 1977	

FIRST EPISODE

First Episode was first performed at the Q Theatre, Kew, London, on 11 September 1933. The cast was as follows:

ALBERT ARNOLD	Max Adrian
PHILIP KAHN	Owen Griffith
TONY WODEHOUSE	Noel Dryden
JOAN TAYLOR	Meriel Forbes-Robertson
DAVID LISTER	Patrick Waddington
MARGOT GRESHAM	Rosalinde Fuller
JAMES	Vincent King
A BULLER	Robert Syers
Director	Muriel Pratt

It subsequently transferred to the Comedy Theatre, London, opening on 19 January 1934, with the following changes to the cast:

PHILIP KAHN	Angus L. MacLeod
TONY WODEHOUSE	William Fox
MARGOT GRESHAM	Barbara Hoffe
A BULLER	Jack Allen

The play received its US premiere at the Ritz Theatre, New York, on 17 September 1934. The cast was as follows:

ALBERT ARNOLD	Max Adrian
PHILIP KAHN	Statts Cotsworth
TONY WODEHOUSE	John Halloran
JOAN TAYLOR	Gerrie Worthing
DAVID LISTER	Patrick Waddington
MARGOT GRESHAM	Leona Maricle
JAMES	Stanley Harrison
A BULLER	T.C. Dunham
Director	Haddon Mason

Characters

ALBERT ARNOLD (BERTIE)
PHILIP KAHN
TONY WODEHOUSE
JOAN TAYLOR
DAVID LISTER
MARGOT GRESHAM
JAMES, *a butler*
A BULLER

ACT ONE

Scene One

*A living room in an undergraduate lodging home. The room
wears an air of comfort and is clearly used by people who are
not scrupulously tidy. The outstanding feature of the room is a
large fireplace in the centre of the book wall. It is flanked on
one side by a large settee. The latter is ultra-modern both in
colour and design, and quite out of keeping with the rest of the
furniture, which is simple and rather old-fashioned. Against the
wall behind the settee is a cabinet containing drinks. On the
other side of the fireplace stand two easy chairs, and on either
side of it on the back wall stand two large bookcases in some
disorder. In the corner upstage is a cabinet gramophone with a
small table beside, on which are strewn numerous records.
Downstage is a plain square table covered with books and a
telephone and a door leading into the bedroom. Upstage is
another door leading to the hall. In the left wall, two large
windows overlook the street. Above the fireplace hangs a
startling Impressionist picture; on the right wall a large
photogravure of the* Relief of Ladysmith, *and on the left wall
two hunting prints. The once fawn-coloured carpet is now dirty
and beer-stained.*

On rise of curtain, ALBERT ARNOLD (BERTIE) *is discovered
sitting facing the audience, at the table, addressing envelopes.
He is fair, with a largish, well-groomed moustache. He works
with an air of great importance.*

Enter PHILIP KAHN, *almost immediately, carrying a gown.*

PHILIP. Hello, Bertie. (*Puts gown down.*)

BERTIE (*without looking up*). Hullo.

> *There is a pause while* BERTIE *continues to address
> envelopes.*

PHILIP. You're very busy.

BERTIE. Yes, I'm working.

Slight pause.

PHILIP. What at?

BERTIE. I've got to send out thousands of tickets for our show. I'm Front of House Manager for the University Dramatic Society this year.

PHILIP. Weren't you Front of House Manager last year?

BERTIE. No, last year I sold programmes.

PHILIP. Congratulations, Bertie. You'll be making quite a name for yourself soon in dramatic circles.

BERTIE. Well, I know it isn't much. But at any rate, it's something.

PHILIP. Why be so modest. What exactly are your duties?

BERTIE. Well – er – I have to send out tickets, and – er – I have to arrange seats. And then, of course, on the night I wear a tailcoat.

PHILIP. And a white tie?

BERTIE (*laughing*). Of course. You don't think I'd wear a black tie with a tailcoat, do you?

PHILIP. No, Bertie. Just my fun.

BERTIE (*slightly offended*). Oh, I see. (*Resumes work.*)

PHILIP. You're doing *Antony and Cleopatra* this year, aren't you?

BERTIE. Yes. (*Condescendingly.*) Shakespeare's best, don't you think?

PHILIP. No. Still, it's quite a good play for children to act. (*Getting drink from sideboard.*)

BERTIE (*offended*). You ought to come and see some of the rehearsals before you say things like that. It's going to be one of the best shows we've ever put on. Margot Gresham is absolutely marvellous. Her name alone is worth a fortune to us.

PHILIP. I'm glad to hear it. (*Assuming the tone of an elderly don.*) Still I cannot say I altogether approve of these undergraduate productions. In my day young men had enough to occupy themselves in their work and their play not to waste their time in such diversions, however innocent they may be. Look at young Tony Wodehouse, for example.

BERTIE. That's not a bad imitation of Tony's tutor. He's always speaking to him like that.

PHILIP. You don't surprise me. After all, his final schools are in a few weeks' time, and he can't be doing much work while he's producing this play of yours – I mean, Shakespeare's. In similar circumstances my own tutor would pass out completely. (*Pensively.*) Poor little man, that would be an entirely new experience for him.

BERTIE. Still, Tony's doing awfully well as producer, and I think the way he is going to play Antony will be marvellous. I never knew he had it in him.

PHILIP. Well – as a producer, he shows genius.

BERTIE. What d'you mean?

PHILIP. Why did he get Joan Taylor to act in the play?

BERTIE (*indignant*). Because she's a jolly good little actress; without much experience, of course; still, it's all there.

PHILIP (*sits on lower window seat*). I'll say it's all there. But not what you mean.

BERTIE (*with dignity*). I don't follow you, I'm afraid.

PHILIP. My dear Bertie, it's perfectly obvious why Tony chose her for the part. She has one of the best figures I've ever seen, but as an actress she's just another good willing girl.

BERTIE (*furious*). Let me tell you, you're quite wrong. I know Tony's reputation with women might make you think that, but Miss Taylor just isn't that sort of girl.

PHILIP. I don't know what sort of girl she is, though I've a good idea. But I do know what sort of actress she is.

BERTIE. How do you know?

PHILIP. Because Tony told me.

BERTIE. What did he say?

PHILIP. He said she was lousy.

BERTIE (*absolutely furious*). Well, if he said that he's more of a cad than I thought he was.

PHILIP. Come, come, Bertie. You are speaking of one who shares the same roof with you.

BERTIE (*recklessly*). I don't care. Just because he's a friend of mine is not going to stop me seeing his faults. I think the way he treats women is perfectly scandalous.

PHILIP. In what way?

BERTIE. Well, this Joan Taylor business, if what you say is true, is a case in point. Taking a young innocent girl, making love to her, trying to seduce her, and then after he's – after he's – he's – er –

PHILIP. Don't say it!

BERTIE. After he's ruined her, casting her away like – er... like –

PHILIP (*suggesting*). A faded bouquet?

BERTIE. Like yesterday's newspaper.

PHILIP. The comparison is unfair. Newspapers have some use after you've read them.

BERTIE (*ignoring him*). Thank heavens Miss Taylor won't stand for anything like that.

PHILIP. Won't she? Are you sure?

BERTIE. Of course I'm sure. You and Tony seem to think that there's no such thing as a good girl nowadays.

PHILIP (*blows down pipe. With scientific detachment*). I believe they do exist. But all the girls I know are over sixteen.

BERTIE. That's the sort of attitude I hate. What'll you do when you get married?

PHILIP. My mother will tell me.

The clock strikes the hour.

BERTIE. No, what I mean is, won't you expect your wife to have been good?

PHILIP. I shall expect her to be as tactful about her past life as I shall be myself about my own.

BERTIE. You mean you wouldn't mind if she's had an affair with other men?

PHILIP. Provided she's not too explicit about them.

BERTIE. I can't understand that point of view. If I found out that my wife was not completely pure, I think I should shoot her.

PHILIP. Thus making an honest woman of her?

BERTIE. Anyway, I shall take good care that the girl I marry is above suspicion.

PHILIP. Be careful she doesn't shoot you, Bertie, when she finds out what your past has been.

BERTIE. I don't know what you mean. I think I can safely say that I've never in all my life given way to sex.

PHILIP. Better touch wood, Bertie.

BERTIE. I can't understand why you and Tony and David are always finding it necessary to mess about with girls.

PHILIP. I can safely say I've never found it necessary to mess about with girls. I hope I don't reach that stage for another sixty years or so.

BERTIE. You three never seem to think of anything but sex all day long. The amount of dirt that's talked in this house is incredible.

PHILIP. Are dirt and sex the same thing?

BERTIE (*ignoring the question*). The whole thing's unhealthy, in my opinion.

Pause.

PHILIP (*slowly*). Bertie, there's one thing that always puzzled me about you, and that's why you came to live in this house.

BERTIE (*looking hurt*). What d'you mean?

PHILIP. I don't want to be rude, but it's always been perfectly obvious that you disapproved violently of almost everything that Tony or I or David ever did. You'd have been far happier in an ordinary undergraduate household.

BERTIE. I knew Tony very well at school. He was quite different then. (*Pause.*) And then I knew all three of you and liked you all. (*Pause. Rather pathetically.*) Of course, it's obvious I don't fit in this house.

PHILIP. Don't be a fool, Bertie, I was only joking.

BERTIE. Oh! (*Pause.*) What's the time, Philip?

PHILIP (*looking at watch*). About twenty-five to twelve.

BERTIE. Good Lord! I've got to get all this stuff finished tonight. (*Indicating envelopes.*) I'll have to work like a nigger to do it. (*Starts to resume work.*)

The door bangs. Enter JOAN TAYLOR and TONY WODEHOUSE.

TONY (*introducing*). Joan, I don't think you know Philip. Miss Taylor – Mr Kahn.

They shake hands.

You know Bertie, of course.

JOAN (*smiling sweetly at* BERTIE). Of course. You're in the show, aren't you?

BERTIE. I'm Front of House Manager.

JOAN. That sounds awfully important.

BERTIE. It is. Aren't you both very tired after rehearsals?

JOAN. Dead beat.

PHILIP. I hope you'll excuse me. I've got to be going. I've got a lot of work to do tonight.

PHILIP *goes to door, sees that* BERTIE *is not following, turns and looks at him meaningly.*

You've got a lot of work to do too, Bertie.

BERTIE *takes no notice, basking in the sunshine of* JOAN'*s smile.*

(*With meaning.*) Bertie! You've got a lot of work to do.

BERTIE. You mean the envelopes, I know.

PHILIP (*desperately*). Well, come upstairs with me and do them, besides, I've got something to show you.

BERTIE (*suspiciously*). What?

Suddenly, BERTIE *grasps* PHILIP'*s meaning and is overcome with embarrassment.*

Oh, yes – of course – I remember – how silly of me.

He takes up the pile of envelopes, and in his confusion drops half of them on the floor. Loses his nerve completely. Gathers up the envelopes and darts for the door, murmuring inaudible apologies.

Exeunt BERTIE *and* PHILIP. JOAN *and* TONY *laugh.* JOAN *comes close to* TONY *and snuggles up to him.*

TONY (*kissing* JOAN). Darling, I thought they'd never go. I've been waiting for that all evening.

JOAN. So have I.

TONY. And I've been waiting for a drink, too. (*Goes to cabinet and pours out a drink.*)

JOAN *sits on sofa and takes up a copy of* Bystander.

JOAN. Oh, Tony, look. Here's a picture of Margot.

TONY. Of *our* Margot? Let's have a look.

He sits beside JOAN *on the sofa and takes paper from her, and looks long and searchingly at the picture.*

Isn't she grand?

JOAN. I think she's gorgeous. I'm so thrilled to be acting in the same play with her.

TONY. Not as thrilled as I am at being her producer.

JOAN. How did you ever get her to come down here? I believe they pay hundreds of pounds a week in London.

TONY (*a little grandly*). Oh, I knew her slightly in town, and when we decided to play *Antony and Cleopatra*, I wrote and asked her if she'd do it. It was a bit of a shock to me when she replied that she would. I've never had an actress as famous as Margot Gresham down here before.

JOAN. Don't you die with fright when you're producing her?

TONY. Yes. Do I show it?

JOAN (*snuggling up to him again*). No. You look ever so stern and nasty when you're producing. Make poor little me quite frightened.

TONY *moves a little away.*

TONY. She's a wonderful actress, don't you think?

JOAN. Yes, she is.

She snuggles up again, and again TONY *moves away.*

TONY. She's got such poise. She seems so sure of herself, somehow.

JOAN (*petulantly*). You'll make me jealous if you go on talking about her like this.

TONY (*kissing her perfunctorily*). Sorry, darling. What shall I talk about?

JOAN. Me. (*Rises, picks up cloak from floor.*)

TONY (*momentarily at a loss*). I think you're the sweetest little girl I know.

JOAN. And I think you're the sweetest little boy I know.

TONY (*jumping up*). Hey! You mustn't say things like that. Do you know who you're talking to?

JOAN. Tony Wodehouse, the great producer. Don't be angry with me, darling. Do you have this lovely room all to yourself?

TONY. No. Four of us live together in this house, and we kind of share it.

JOAN. Oh. I suppose those two that were in here when we came in live with you?

TONY. Yes.

JOAN. Who's the other one?

TONY. David Lister. I don't think you've met him.

JOAN. Oh, I've heard all about him. You and he are great chums, aren't you?

TONY. No, darling, we're just great friends.

JOAN. I should love to meet him.

TONY. You will, I expect. He'll be in here tonight.

JOAN. I wish I was at the *Varsity*. (*Wistfully*.) You must have such larks together, you four.

TONY (*wincing*). Heaven forbid!

JOAN (*emitting a high trill of laughter*). Oh, don't be so soft, Tony, you know what I mean.

TONY. Yes, I know what you mean, darling. (*Goes to gramophone, puts on a record and turns to* JOAN.) Show me that step.

JOAN *goes to him. They dance a little. Suddenly* JOAN *stops dancing, still in his arms, and looks up at him.*

JOAN. Are you coming to see me at The King's Head, darling?

TONY. Do you really want me to?

JOAN. Of course I want you to. Don't *you* want to?

TONY. If the Proctors catch me out after twelve o'clock I'd get sent down. I can't afford to take unnecessary risks just now.

JOAN (*petulantly*). Of course, if you'd rather not come...

TONY. Joan, you know there's nothing I would like better.

JOAN. Do come soon, darling.

They kiss. While they are kissing, DAVID LISTER *enters. They do not notice him. He goes to the gramophone and stops it.* JOAN *and* TONY *jump apart.*

DAVID. I'm sorry but I hate that tune.

TONY. Oh, hullo, David. (*After a moment's confusion.*) I don't think you've met each other. This is Miss Taylor – Mr Lister.

JOAN. Oh, dear, it's so awful being caught like that. What will you think of me, Mr Lister?

DAVID. How d'you mean – 'caught'? All I saw was your teaching Tony a new step.

JOAN (*laughing shrilly*). Yes, that's what I was doing, wasn't it, Tony?

TONY (*at the drink cabinet*). Yes, that's all.

DAVID (*to* JOAN). It looked a nice step. You must teach it to me some time.

JOAN. Oh, I'd love to – David. You mustn't mind my calling you David, but Tony has told me so much about you it's as if we'd been friends for years. He's just said that you and he were the most tremendous chums.

TONY, *standing behind* JOAN, *makes an apologetic gesture to* DAVID.

DAVID. That was very nice of him. He's told me a lot about you too. (*Sits at a chair above the table.*)

TONY *hands* DAVID *a drink.*

Thanks, Tony.

TONY. I seem to have been doing a lot of talking recently.

DAVID (*to* JOAN). Aren't you drinking?

JOAN. I don't drink, thanks.

TONY. Don't you believe her, David. Tonight at the rehearsal she put down seven ginger beers, one on top of the other, and she didn't turn a hair.

DAVID. What else didn't she do?

TONY. You'd be surprised.

JOAN. Tony, you are – (*To* DAVID). I only drank three, David. Tony's such a fibber.

DAVID. Don't worry, Joan. I wouldn't believe such a thing of you. Tony fibs like mad. I'm always catching him at it.

JOAN. Isn't it awful!

She comes up to DAVID *and takes his tie in her hand. It is a blue tie with white feathers.*

What a funny tie. Does it mean anything?

She is very close to DAVID. *He seems very conscious of this, and doesn't answer at once.*

What are those funny little things? They're feathers, aren't they?

DAVID. Er – yes – it's the Pacifist Club. I'm President of it.

JOAN *looks bewildered.*

TONY. D'you know what a pacifist is, darling?

JOAN. Oh, yes. I'm one myself.

DAVID. Splendid.

JOAN (*referring to the tie*). I'm always looking on the dark side of things.

TONY. You're thinking of a pessimist, darling.

JOAN. Oh, am I? How silly.

DAVID. A pacifist is someone who is trying to prevent another war.

JOAN (*rather doubtfully*). Oh! Then is that all the tie means?

DAVID. Yes.

JOAN. Well, I always say that that sort of thing is all right in peacetime, but that if there was a war we'd all have to do our bit, if you know what I mean.

TONY. I know what you mean.

JOAN. I mean, I should do my bit.

DAVID. I'm sure you would.

BERTIE *suddenly pushes his head around the door, and, seeing that all is clear, he comes in, followed by* PHILIP.

BERTIE. I say, you don't mind if I use the phone, do you? I forgot to ask Marg how many seats she wanted for the first night.

TONY. You mean Miss Gresham, don't you?

BERTIE. Yes. Her friends call her Marg, you know.

TONY. I didn't know.

JOAN. I've got an idea. Why not ask her to come around here, we'll have a little party.

All except TONY *give signs of assent.*

TONY. It's much too late – she'd have to go at twelve, anyway. It must be nearly that now – besides, she'll never come.

JOAN. Oh, I'm sure she would. She's such a sport.

DAVID. There's no harm in asking her, anyway, I'm longing to meet her.

PHILIP. So am I.

JOAN. Well then, let's. Ask her, Bertie.

BERTIE *has been dialling a number. He now speaks into the phone.*

TONY. There's not a chance of her coming.

PHILIP. She'll come all right if Bertie asks her.

DAVID. Why? Has she a secret passion for him?

PHILIP. Yes. Didn't you know? Apparently she never takes her eyes off him whenever he's near her.

DAVID. I see. She gives him that hungry look that seems to strip him of all his clothes and lay him naked before her. I've read about it in books.

BERTIE. I say, shut up your chaps, I can't hear. (*Into phone.*) Hullo, is that The King's Head Hotel? Will you put me through to Miss Margot Gresham, please.

TONY. It's quite crazy. What's the use of asking her round here this time of night?

DAVID. I don't see why she shouldn't come. Just for a few minutes, anyway.

BERTIE (*into phone*). Hullo! Is that Marg – I mean, Margot – I mean, Miss Gresham? (*Loses his nerve completely and signals to* JOAN.)

JOAN comes and takes the receiver from his hand and speaks through phone.

JOAN. Hullo, Margot. This is Joan speaking… Margot, we're having a party… an awfully jolly little party… do come and join us for a few minutes. It's only a step from the hotel… Tony Wodehouse is here… yes… and Bertie… you know him, don't you?… Oh, you don't… I thought you did… he wears spectacles… surely you've seen them at rehearsals… yes, that's right… large ones. I'll send him around to fetch you if you like… yes, right now… Cheers. (*Puts down receiver.*) The spectacles did it, she's coming. Bertie, you've got to go and fetch her… tout suite.

BERTIE (*with impressive nonchalance*). All right. As I'm the only one who seems to know her, except Tony, I suppose I'd better.

They all hurry him off, showing great excitement. Exit BERTIE.

TONY. We'd better tidy the place up a bit before she comes.

He is very nervous, and attempts to put a very disordered room in order.

JOAN. And I must go and powder my nose. (*Looks enquiringly round.*)

PHILIP. Oh, I'll show you, if you like.

DAVID goes and opens the door, and JOAN exits. PHILIP is about to follow her, but DAVID stops him and shuts door after JOAN.

DAVID. Now, then, you go up and tell James we want some glasses and siphons.

Exit PHILIP. DAVID and TONY are left alone. DAVID sits, while TONY is fussing nervously around the room.

Tony, what a grand little girl.

TONY (*absently*). Who?

DAVID. Joan Taylor, of course.

TONY. D'you really think so?

DAVID (*surprised*). Why, don't you? I thought she was your particular cup of tea.

TONY. Oh, she's all right. I wish she wasn't so dumb, that's all.

DAVID. Well, what d' you expect for your money? She's got one of the best figures I've ever seen.

TONY. Body, body, body. That's all you ever think about in women.

DAVID. What else is there to think about in women?

TONY. The mind, of course. Don't you ever think of the spiritual side of women?

DAVID. Spiritual Nerts!

TONY. The trouble with you is that you've got no soul.

DAVID. Tony, you're drunk.

TONY. I'm as sober as you are.

DAVID. Then what's the matter with you? Don't say you've fallen in love.

TONY. Certainly not. What a damned silly idea.

DAVID. Is it Margot Gresham?

TONY. Don't be a fool, David.

DAVID. Yes, it is. Ever since you knew she was coming round here, you've been bobbing about like an agitated hen. For God's sake, sit down, you're getting on my nerves.

TONY. You're right, it is Margot Gresham. David, she's unlike any other woman I've ever met.

DAVID. In what way?

TONY. Well, she's the first woman I've ever met whose mind I could admire.

DAVID. Are you talking about a woman with a mind? It's a contradiction in terms.

TONY. I thought that once; I don't now. You'll love her, David, when you meet her. You haven't met her, have you?

DAVID. No, but I've seen her on the stage.

TONY. Don't you think she's grand?

DAVID. She's all right, but she's practically in her dotage.

TONY. What do you mean? She can't be more than thirty-five.

DAVID. That's old enough, isn't it?

TONY. 'Old'! Why, at thirty-five a woman is just reaching the prime of life.

DAVID. Is that what she told you?

TONY. Don't be a fool, David. She wouldn't care if you did think her old.

Enter JOAN *and* PHILIP.

JOAN. Hasn't Margot come yet?

PHILIP *puts glasses, etc., on the sideboard.*

TONY. Not yet.

PHILIP. Is the stage all set for Her Majesty's arrival?

DAVID. All but the red carpet. We haven't had time for that.

A ring is heard.

TONY (*excited*). That'll be her.

PHILIP. What is the procedure? Do we all sink down in a deep curtsy as she comes in?

DAVID. I've forgotten how to curtsy.

JOAN. I never learnt.

TONY (*suddenly*). Good Lord! Supposing she doesn't drink whisky. That's all we've got.

DAVID. There ought to be some gin there as well.

TONY. There isn't. We finished it this morning.

PHILIP. There's some in my room. I'll go and get it.

As PHILIP *is turning to go, the door opens in and* MARGOT GRESHAM *enters, followed by* BERTIE.

BERTIE. And so I said to her, it's better to be good-looking than good.

MARGOT. That was brilliant of you.

BERTIE (*enjoying himself as Master of Ceremonies*). Let me see, you know Joan and Tony, of course.

MARGOT (*smiling at them*). Of course.

BERTIE. And Mr Kahn – Miss Gresham.

PHILIP *and* MARGOT *shake hands.*

This is Mr Lister – Miss Gresham.

DAVID *and* MARGOT *shake hands. There is an awkward pause after this.*

MARGOT (*breaking in*). What a nice room. Who does it belong to. You, Tony?

TONY. No, it doesn't belong to anybody really. I mean, we all share it.

MARGOT. That must be nice. What a lovely sofa.

PHILIP. That belongs to Tony.

TONY. Do sit down.

MARGOT *sits on sofa*.

Can I get you something to drink?

MARGOT. Yes, thanks. I think I'll have a little – (*Considering*.) a little whisky.

TONY (*with relief*). Thanks. I'll get you some. (*Goes to cabinet to get whisky*.)

DAVID, PHILIP *and* BERTIE *surround the sofa*, BERTIE *sitting on it next to* MARGOT.

BERTIE. How do you like the town, Miss Gresham?

MARGOT. I love it. I've always wanted to act down here.

Pause.

DAVID. How's the production going? Is Tony any good at producing Shakespeare?

MARGOT. I think they're both good.

DAVID. Ye gods, some praise – and how does he play Antony?

MARGOT. I feel an incapable Cleopatra.

Pause.

PHILIP. I suppose this is the first time you've ever acted in an amateur production?

MARGOT. Yes. I've never done it before.

BERTIE. Lucky amateurs. I wish I wasn't only the manager.

TONY *comes to them with* MARGOT*'s drink. He kicks* BERTIE *on the shin and jerks his thumb, indicating that he wants to sit where* BERTIE *is sitting.* BERTIE *reluctantly gives way, and* TONY *sits beside* MARGOT.

Pause.

TONY. How do you like the town, Miss Gresham?

MARGOT. Lord, you're not going to start that, I hope. Why does everybody treat me as if I was some monstrous old dowager duchess?

The others in the room are taking no interest in this conversation and are talking quietly amongst themselves.

Everybody I meet asks me the same question: 'How d'you like the town, Miss Gresham?' The next time somebody asks me that I'm just going to answer – 'I think it's lousy.'

They laugh.

TONY. Seriously, though, I rather feel I'm responsible for dragging you down here. I do hope you're not having too frightful a time.

MARGOT. Of course I'm not. I'm loving every minute of it.

TONY. I was telling Joan – (*Signals to* JOAN.) or – Miss Taylor, you know – what a wonderful surprise it was when I got your letter saying you were coming down here. I never thought you would for a moment. I can't tell you how grateful I am.

MARGOT. There's nothing to be grateful for. I was only too glad to come down here to act.

DAVID. Do you prefer the films or the stage, Miss Gresham?

MARGOT. Come now, that's only a little better than asking me how I like the town.

DAVID. I'm sorry.

BERTIE. Anyway, everyone knows that Miss Gresham prefers the films.

MARGOT. As a matter of fact, I prefer the stage.

TONY. I'm glad. I loved your last play.

MARGOT. Did you? Very few other people seemed to.

TONY. I saw it three times.

MARGOT. Three times? Why?

TONY. I don't know.

BERTIE. He went to see you, you know, not the play.

TONY *glares at* BERTIE.

Yes, he wrote you a letter once.

TONY *kicks* BERTIE *desperately.*

MARGOT (*to* TONY). Really? Did I answer it?

TONY. I got a photograph signed 'Yours sincerely, Margot Gresham'.

BERTIE. Yes, he always said it was signed by your secretary.

MARGOT (*to* TONY). How dare you suggest such a thing. Have you still got it? I'd rather like to see it.

TONY *pulls out a photograph.*

DAVID. There's devotion for you, Miss Gresham. I hope you find it touching

MARGOT. I do. (*Takes photo.*) But that's one of our Class B.

TONY. 'Class B'?

MARGOT. We only send that to people who don't enclose a stamped and addressed envelope.

DAVID. Did he sink as low as that?

MARGOT. It looks like it. (*To* TONY.) Very thoughtless of you, costing me a penny halfpenny.

BERTIE. Next time he'd better enclose two stamped envelopes to make up for it. (*Roars with laughter.*)

MARGOT. I'll give you a proper photograph, if you'd like one. Remind me and I'll bring one round to the rehearsal tomorrow.

TONY. That'll be marvellous.

BERTIE. Will you give me one, too, Miss Gresham?

MARGOT (*handing him the photo*). You can have this one.

TONY (*snatching it back from* BERTIE). Oh, no, he can't. I wouldn't part with that.

MARGOT (*to* BERTIE). I'll send you one from town.

BERTIE. Oh, thank you. I should love one. I've always been a great fan of yours, too, you know. You mustn't think that Tony's your only admirer. I thought your performance in *Othello* was absolutely marvellous.

MARGOT. I wasn't in *Othello*. I've never acted in Shakespeare before coming down here, you know.

BERTIE. Oh, haven't you? I must be mixing you up with someone else. Of course, acting in Shakespeare's entirely different to any other sort of acting, don't you think? I know from my own experience how difficult it is. When I played the name part in *Julius Caesar* immediately after acting in *Charley's Aunt*, I found...

TONY. Bertie, you might get me another drink, will you?

BERTIE. Oh, all right.

PHILIP *is sitting at the piano, playing*.

MARGOT. Thanks for getting rid of that menace.

DAVID *crosses to* PHILIP *at piano*.

TONY. It was a pleasure.

MARGOT. Did he play Julius Caesar?

TONY. Yes, at school.

MARGOT. Good?

TONY. Oh, he didn't have anything to say. He only appeared as the corpse in the funeral scene.

MARGOT. I should think he'd make a good corpse.

TONY (*catching sight of her wristwatch*). I say, is that the right time?

MARGOT (*looking at her wristwatch*). Yes. Why?

TONY. It means you've got to go, I'm afraid.

MARGOT. Why, do they turn us out at twelve o'clock?

TONY. University rules. I'm terribly sorry to have got you round here, and then turn you out after a few minutes like this.

MARGOT. It doesn't matter. I must come earlier another night, that's all.

TONY. It's such a shame, because I wanted to – er – I wanted to discuss that scene with you tonight.

MARGOT. Which scene?

TONY. The love scene.

Pause.

(*Suddenly.*) I say, couldn't you come back here tonight after the others are gone?

MARGOT. Why, I don't understand. How can I?

TONY (*urging*). It's perfectly easy. All you've got to do is to climb through the window.

MARGOT. You won't catch me climbing through any windows.

TONY (*with insistence*). But it's really awfully easy. You just *walk* through it, and I'll be here to help you.

MARGOT. But surely the scene can wait until tomorrow morning?

TONY. I won't have any time tomorrow morning. Do please come back tonight.

MARGOT. Shall I? What will your friends think?

TONY. Oh, I'll get rid of them.

MARGOT *gives* TONY *a look.*

I mean – we must be alone to rehearse. Do say you'll come.

DAVID *begins to sing to* PHILIP's *accompaniment. After the song,* DAVID *crosses to* TONY *and* MARGOT.

DAVID. Now, then, Tony, I want to talk to Miss Gresham before she goes. Please don't go for a minute.

TONY (*to* MARGOT). Will you excuse me. (*Joins the others*.)

DAVID *sits with* MARGOT.

MARGOT. What a charming boy he is.

DAVID. He's very young, don't you think?

MARGOT (*laughing*). But aren't you very young, too?

DAVID. Compared to him, I feel very old. Age isn't only a matter of years.

MARGOT (*smiling*). I'm glad to hear it. You're great friends, aren't you?

DAVID. Tony and I? Yes, we are.

MARGOT. He's told me a lot about you.

DAVID. He's told me a lot about you, too.

MARGOT. Really! What has he said?

DAVID. He told me tonight that you were the first woman he had ever met whose mind he could admire.

MARGOT. What does he mean by 'mind'?

DAVID. Not brains. I suppose he means he's never met any woman, that's to say until he met you, whom he could bear as a companion.

MARGOT. That's rather a depressing view of my sex, isn't it. How did he get it?

DAVID. I'm afraid he learnt it from me.

MARGOT. Are you a woman-hater, then?

DAVID. No, just the reverse.

MARGOT. I see. (*Pause*.) I suppose you have a great influence over Tony?

DAVID. I suppose I have. He needs someone to take care of him. He's very weak, you know.

MARGOT. I didn't know, as a matter of fact.

DAVID. Well, I suppose 'weak' wasn't quite the right word. He's impressionable.

MARGOT. Most young men are.

DAVID. I'm not.

MARGOT. Yes, but you've just said that you're not young.

DAVID. I should hate you to think of me as a dirty old man, though.

MARGOT. But that's what you are according to your own confession.

DAVID. I was only speaking comparatively when I said I was old, and I never said I was dirty.

MARGOT. Perhaps my womanly intuition has played me false.

DAVID. I hope so. That's what womanly intuition generally does.

MARGOT. You're a cynic, aren't you?

DAVID. I suppose so.

MARGOT. It's a funny friendship between you and Tony. He's a sentimentalist, isn't he?

DAVID. I didn't think so until tonight.

MARGOT. The friendship of young men can be very selfish.

DAVID. But so impregnable.

JOAN. Margot, Bertie's going to sing to us.

BERTIE. Oh, no, I couldn't.

DAVID. Do, Bertie.

BERTIE. But I don't know anything.

PHILIP. You know *Madame Butterfly*. I heard you singing it in your bath this morning.

BERTIE. That was 'Stormy Weather'.

MARGOT. Well, let's hear that, anyway.

TONY. You don't know what you're letting yourself in for, Miss Gresham.

DAVID. I think on the whole, Bertie, your rendering of 'Young and Healthy' is better.

PHILIP strikes up 'Young and Healthy' on the piano. After a lot of persuasion, BERTIE *delivers the first two lines.*

Enter JAMES. *He is the butler-landlord.*

JAMES. It's after twelve. I'm afraid the ladies must go.

JOAN. Oh, what a shame. Must we go?

JAMES. I'm afraid so, miss. University rules.

JOAN. But can't we stay just a little bit longer?

JAMES. Sorry, miss. It'd be as much as my place is worth to let you stay.

JOAN. You must finish that song some other evening, Bertie. It has great possibilities.

TONY. Will you come back?

MARGOT. In ten minutes?

TONY. Not a minute longer.

MARGOT. Come on, Joan.

The two girls collect their things, and exeunt, followed by the four boys. 'Goodnights', etc., can be heard outside in the passage, then the sound of a door closing. TONY *re-enters first, very excited. Then* PHILIP *and* BERTIE *enter.*

TONY (*going to the table and fussing about with books*). I say, d'you mind very much going next door? I've got a hell of a lot of work to do tonight.

PHILIP. No, that's all right. I'm going to bed, anyway. Goodnight.

Exit PHILIP.

BERTIE. I'm going to bed. (*Stops at door.*) I say, isn't she a topper?

TONY. Who?

BERTIE. Margot, of course. I mean, she's so easy to get on with, don't you think?

TONY. Go away, Bertie, that's a good fellow.

BERTIE. Oh, all right. Cheer-ho!

Exit BERTIE. TONY *starts to put the room in order, but hurriedly stops as* DAVID *enters and goes to mantelpiece for pipe.* TONY *goes to table and starts with books, as before.*

TONY. David, d'you mind going next door? I've got an essay to write tonight.

DAVID *sits in easy chair.*

DAVID. Why are you writing an essay tonight when your tutorial's on Tuesday?

TONY. My tutorial's been changed to tomorrow.

DAVID (*settling down*). All right, go ahead. I won't disturb you.

TONY. Yes, you will. Do go into the next room, there's a good chap.

DAVID (*completely settling down*). I'll be as quiet as a mouse.

TONY. I can never write an essay when there's someone in the room.

DAVID. Nonsense, I'll be able to help you. What's the essay about?

TONY. It's on something you know nothing about.

DAVID. What?

TONY. Constitutional law.

DAVID. But I'm one of the world's greatest authorities on constitutional law. You mean to say you haven't read my little handbook – *Lister's Constitutional Law in a Nutshell*?

TONY. I never heard anyone talk as much rot as you. For God's sake, go away. Can't you see I want to do some work?

DAVID. Go ahead. I'm not stopping you.

Short pause.

I feel I want to lie here and muse on life and the mutability of human affairs.

TONY (*with a look at the window*). Can't you do that in bed?

DAVID. I can never muse in bed. I always fall asleep.

TONY. I wish to God you'd find some other place to muse in.

Pause.

TONY *is in despair of ever getting rid of* DAVID.

DAVID. What a figure that girl has!

TONY. Who? Margot?

DAVID (*contemptuously*). Margot? That old relic? No, Joan, of course.

TONY. Oh, Joan.

DAVID. Oh, youth – fickle, fickle youth – why you were mad about her a few days ago, and now it's – (*Mimicking him.*) 'Oh – Joan.'

TONY. David – *will you go to bed.*

DAVID (*sitting up*). Is this a sudden dislike for my company – or do I scent an intrigue?

Pause.

TONY (*simply*). Look here, Margot Gresham's coming back.

DAVID. What?

TONY. Margot Gresham's coming back.

DAVID. Whose suggestion was that? Hers?

TONY. Mine.

DAVID. Then she must be a quick thinker. Are you going to give her the works?

TONY (*with dignity*). We're going to rehearse a scene from the play.

DAVID. Then you won't mind me staying to watch.

TONY. Yes, I will.

DAVID. Seriously, though, Tony, I don't think you'll have any success with her.

TONY. I don't want any success with her.

DAVID. Then why did you ask her to come back? I know perfectly well it wasn't to rehearse.

TONY. Oh, I don't know. Just want to talk to her, I suppose.

DAVID. Nothing else?

TONY. There you go again – body, body, body –

DAVID. Well, it seems a queer sort of pleasure having a woman back at this time of night just to talk to her.

TONY. She's worth talking to, David. She's got a mind.

DAVID. I know. I know, I've heard all that. I suppose you know best what you want. Now if it was Joan Taylor you'd asked back, I'd understand perfectly. And do you realise that for a moment tonight I felt guilty because I'd broken the tenth commandment.

TONY. Only the tenth?

DAVID. Yes, you know the one that goes – 'Thou shall not covet thy neighbour's ox or cow', and when I looked at your Joan, I felt guilty.

TONY. Do you want to have an affair with Joan?

DAVID. Do ducks want to swim?

TONY. Well, it's a long time since I gave you a present – you can have her.

DAVID. Thanks, old boy, and do I get the pound of tea as well?

TONY. Seriously, I'm through. I did think I was keen on Joan once, but now –

DAVID (*rises*). Since the quick worker has come on the scene, you're sunk.

TONY *pushes him to the door.*

Oh, goodnight, Romeo. Be careful – a little wine and a lot of woman – how does it go?

TONY. I don't know, but out *you* go. (*Pushes him through the door.*)

Exit DAVID.

Phew! (*Fixes lights and cushions, etc.*)

There is a tap at the window.

(*Leaning out.*) Just a minute.

MARGOT *enters through the window. Distant music from a gramophone, off.*

MARGOT. Well, I've never made an entrance through a window before.

TONY. I'm so glad you're here. I was afraid you weren't coming.

MARGOT. I said I would.

TONY. I know, but I was afraid you would change your mind.

MARGOT. I'm a woman of my word. I promised.

She shuts the window.

TONY. Then I hope you remember the other promise you made me tonight.

MARGOT. Was there another one?

TONY. The photograph.

MARGOT. Oh, of course. I won't forget that.

TONY. I hope you won't write 'Yours sincerely' on it this time.

MARGOT. What would you like me to write on it?

TONY. Just – 'To Tony'.

MARGOT. 'With love'?

TONY. That's more than I can hope for, but it would be grand.

MARGOT. Everyone gone to bed?

TONY. Yes.

MARGOT. How exciting – alone in a man's rooms after midnight. (*Sits on the sofa and puts her legs up.*)

TONY. Do you know, it seems incredible that you should be sitting there.

MARGOT. Why? Is it a reserved enclosure?

TONY. I'm serious. In the days when I used to go to all your plays and all your films, and wrote to you for photographs, it never occurred to me that you were the sort of person one could meet and talk to just like anyone else.

MARGOT. Why not, Tony? Am I so different from anybody else?

TONY. Oh, yes. You seemed so far away. I used to picture myself rescuing you from perilous situations, but I never pictured you quietly sitting and talking on the sofa in my room.

MARGOT. Tony, do many women sit quietly on your sofa in your rooms after midnight?

TONY. Oh, no.

MARGOT. Really, Tony?

TONY. Of course not.

MARGOT. But I thought that you and Joan – Well, perhaps I shouldn't say it –

TONY. I've always looked on Joan as a sort of – er – sister.

MARGOT. Oh, Tony, you are a joy.

TONY. I don't suppose you remember the first time I met you, do you?

MARGOT. No, Tony, when was that?

TONY. It was at a party in London. I didn't know you were going to be there, and when I saw you I was so frightened I wanted to run away. Finally, I plucked up courage and asked someone to introduce me to you. Don't you remember?

MARGOT. It's hateful of me, but I don't.

TONY. I'd prepared a little speech in case I ever *should* meet you, but I was so nervous I forgot it. You must have thought me a complete halfwit.

MARGOT. No. It's awfully hard to think of something to say when one's first introduced.

TONY. Yes, but I'd prepared so many brilliant things to say, and to forget them was tragic.

MARGOT. Poor Tony! I wish I'd known.

TONY. I can recite my opening speech now, if you like.

MARGOT. Can you? All right, go ahead.

TONY. Well, I was going to say – 'Miss Gresham, I've always been one of your greatest admirers. I thought your performance in *Old Oak Tree* was superb.'

MARGOT. That wouldn't have been very brilliant.

TONY. That was only a start. The brilliant things were going to come out later in the general conversation. We were going to talk about everything, art, literature, life, and I was going to overwhelm you with a flood of epigrams.

MARGOT. What did you actually say?

TONY. 'Good afternoon, Miss Gresham.'

They both laugh.

And I was frightened to death. (*Puts his hand on her knee.*)

MARGOT. You're not frightened now, are you?

TONY. Just a little.

MARGOT. Tony, why?

TONY. I'm so afraid you'll be annoyed with me.

MARGOT. What for?

TONY. For saying all that I have to you.

MARGOT. Don't be silly, Tony! I like it.

TONY. Well, then, I'm frightened you'll be bored.

MARGOT. Bored? Why should I be?

TONY. Because one is bound to be boring, when one is making an effort to attract someone.

MARGOT. Are you making an effort to attract me?

TONY. Haven't you noticed it?

Pause.

MARGOT. Yes, perhaps I have, but I didn't find it boring.

TONY. But so many people must say to you exactly what I've been saying.

MARGOT. They don't all say it so nicely.

TONY. You're not just being kind to me, are you? Or laughing at me?

MARGOT. No, of course not, Tony.

Pause.

TONY. Why did you come back here tonight?

MARGOT. Because you asked me to. We were going to rehearse a scene from the play, weren't we?

TONY. But you know that wasn't the real reason I asked you to come back, didn't you?

MARGOT (*playfully*). Don't say you've brought me here under false pretences. What was the real reason?

TONY. Just to be alone with you and talk to you.

MARGOT. I see.

TONY. You're not angry, are you?

MARGOT (*smiling*). Furious.

TONY. But you know that I didn't really want to rehearse that scene, didn't you?

MARGOT. Of course I did, Tony.

TONY. Then why *did* you come back here?

MARGOT. I don't know. Perhaps for the same reason that you asked me to.

TONY. Oh, Margot, it's not possible…

MARGOT. I said, 'perhaps', Tony.

TONY. I think you're laughing at me.

MARGOT. I'm not, really I'm not.

TONY. Oh, you're wonderful. (*At her feet.*)

MARGOT. How old are you, Tony?

TONY. Twenty.

MARGOT. Do you know how old I am?

TONY. What does that matter?

MARGOT. I don't know. It may matter a lot. I've never felt old till this moment.

TONY. Nonsense.

MARGOT. It isn't nonsense. You're so young, Tony. You're all so very young. It's – it's almost stifling, the atmosphere of youth in this place. It depresses me terribly sometimes.

TONY (*puzzled*). Why?

MARGOT (*laughing*). It's not your fault, Tony – it's mine. A woman of my age should keep away from a university town.

TONY. What d'you mean, a woman of your age? You're not very much older than I am.

MARGOT (*laughing*). Tony, you'll make a wonderful lover one day. I almost envy the girl you'll fall in love with, or perhaps you're in love now?

TONY. I am.

MARGOT. Who with?

TONY. I don't think I can tell you.

MARGOT. Why not?

TONY. Well – you know her.

MARGOT. Do I? Let me guess. Is it Joan?

TONY. No.

MARGOT. Is it anyone in the company?

TONY. Yes.

MARGOT. Oh, who is it, then?

TONY. Margot – please –

MARGOT. Tell me, Tony, do.

TONY. Oh, Margot, it's you. (*Kisses her.*)

MARGOT. This isn't love, Tony.

TONY. What is it, then?

MARGOT. I don't know.

TONY. Oh, I do love you, Margot.

MARGOT. How many other women have you said that to?

TONY. What does it matter about them? I've never felt anything like this before.

   TONY *kisses* MARGOT. *She gets up.*

MARGOT. But there have been other women, haven't there?

TONY. No.

MARGOT (*smiling*). Liar!

TONY. None that matter, anyway.

MARGOT. Why didn't they matter?

TONY. Because I wasn't in love with any of them. I was only attracted.

MARGOT. But you told them you were in love with them?

TONY. I didn't mean it.

MARGOT. Then how do I know you mean it now when you say you're in love with me?

TONY. You must believe it, Margot.

MARGOT. Did these other women believe it?

TONY. Please stop talking about other women. You're so entirely different to them all. Oh, Margot, I do love you. (*Kiss*.)

MARGOT. Oh, Tony, and you say you're only twenty. I must go.

TONY. Oh, no, please stay.

MARGOT. Can I get out by the door now?

TONY. Yes, James will have gone to bed. (*At door*.) Margot, you're terribly angry with me, aren't you?

MARGOT. I'm not, Tony, that's the awful thing. (*Kisses him lightly*.) Goodnight.

TONY *goes out with* MARGOT, *and then returns immediately. He puts on the gramophone. Takes* MARGOT'*s photo from his pocket and props it up on the table. Lights a cigarette, draws a chair facing the photo and sits, smoking and gazing at the photo.*

Enter DAVID *in pyjamas and dressing gown.* TONY *hasn't heard him come in.* DAVID *stands behind* TONY'*s chair.*

DAVID. Her eyes are too close together.

TONY (*turning round*). Hello, David. I thought you'd gone to bed.

DAVID. Her mouth is too small, and I don't like her voice. Did you have a good rehearsal?

TONY (*vaguely*). 'Rehearsal'? Oh, yes, very good.

DAVID. Well, don't stop up too late. (*Going to door*.) And let me give you a piece of advice. Snap out of it.

Exit DAVID.

TONY *remains gazing at photo*.

Curtain.

ACT TWO

Scene One

Same as previous scene, two weeks later, about 11:30 a.m. On rise of curtain, TONY *and* DAVID *are discovered bending over a morning paper which is spread out on the table.* PHILIP *is at the telephone.*

PHILIP (*into phone*). Will you read that telegram over, please?

TONY. There is a horse running today called Cissy; I think I shall back it for sentimental reasons.

PHILIP (*into phone*). No. Lister is the name. Lister – L for Lulu – I for Isidor – S for Stoat – T for Tomboy – E – Erotic – and R for Roundhouse. Have you got that? Now will you take another telegram. Just a minute, please – (*To* TONY.) What was the name of that horse? Cissy, was it? Shall I back it for you?

TONY. Yes, put a pound on for me. It won't win.

PHILIP (*into phone*). Hullo, telegrams. This is to Peekaboo, Newmarket. No, Peekaboo; can't you speak English? Yes, that's right, Peekaboo, Newmarket. Five pounds win Orion, Bellicose two pounds double. One pound win Cissy. This signed Kahn. K – A – H – N. Will you read that, please… Yes, that's right. Thank you. (*Puts down receiver.*)

TONY (*looking through newspaper*). It's do or die for me today, boys. If I don't win about eight pounds today, I'm down the drain.

DAVID. Is that what you owe your bookmaker?

TONY. More or less.

DAVID. If you didn't spend so much money on your women friends, you might be able to pay some of your debts.

TONY. That's not very nice, coming from you.

DAVID. Don't be a fool. You know I didn't mean anything personal.

PHILIP (*who has been opening letters*). Here's a circular from old Blake the bookmaker offering sixty-six to one on Star of Africa for the Derby. He says his promise holds good until tomorrow morning.

DAVID. That's funny. (*Looks at the paper.*) It won the Derby trial stakes at Lingfield yesterday. The price must have shortened a good deal. Yes, here it is. Twenty-two to one.

PHILIP. Listen, boys. I've got a marvellous idea. We can all make fortunes out of this.

TONY. How?

PHILIP. Well, Blake is offering sixty-six to one, while the market price is twenty-two to one; if we put on one hundred pounds with Blake we win six thousand, six hundred if Star of Africa wins.

TONY. Yes, but we lose a hundred if it loses.

PHILIP. Oh, no, we don't. We lay it off at twenty-two's and we make a hundred pounds if it loses and sixteen hundred if it wins. Are you both in on this?

TONY. You can count me in. Can't we do it for more?

PHILIP. I don't know what's to stop us.

DAVID. I can't see any flaw in the scheme, unless this bookmaker lets us down.

PHILIP. Blake's always paid up before.

TONY. Oh, he's all right; besides, we could put him out of business if he didn't pay up. Let's do it for more.

DAVID. I don't think we ought to risk more than a hundred. You can count me in for thirty-three.

PHILIP. All right, but I think before we do anything definite I'll go and see the proprietor of my garage, he used to be a bookmaker, you know. He'll tell me if it's all right.

PHILIP *goes out*.

TONY. I hope this scheme's all right. I could do with the money just now.

Enter BERTIE. *He is carrying a gown and books under his arm.* TONY *and* DAVID *take no notice of him.*

(*Picking up the* Sporting Life.) I might have a few more bets today. (*Looks through the card.*)

BERTIE. You're gambling again, I see.

They appear not to notice him.

Well, I think you're very silly; not that there is anything immoral about gambling, in moderation, of course.

TONY (*to* DAVID). Of course, I might mix double on Gordon Richard's mounts, but then he had four winners yesterday.

BERTIE. I might even have a small bet on the Derby myself this year. It's only when you gamble every day, like you do, that it's foolish.

TONY. What do you think about mix doubling favourites, David?

DAVID. Oh, I should leave it, Tony. You've got a lot of money on already.

BERTIE (*disapproving*). And what horse is going to win you money today?

TONY. You want a horse to back, do you?

BERTIE. Certainly not.

TONY. Well, in case you change your mind, there's a horse called Cissy might suit you.

BERTIE (*huffily*). Don't be funny.

DAVID. I should back it if I were you, Bertie.

BERTIE. Why?

DAVID. You'll be needing the money if you go for many more of those walks down the high street with Joan Taylor.

BERTIE. Are you insinuating that Miss Taylor is the sort of girl who… Anyway, how did you know I went for a walk with her?

DAVID. I know more than you think, Bertie. My spies are everywhere. I know, for instance, that in the cinema yesterday you thrust your foul intentions upon the girl by playing with her, the game known as 'Footie-Footie'.

BERTIE. It's a lie. (*With dignity.*) I have never played 'Footie-Footie' with Miss Taylor, or any other girl.

TONY (*looking up from his paper*). And you call yourself a man!

DAVID. Do you mean to say you took Joan Taylor to a cinema just to see a film? I wonder she didn't slap your face.

BERTIE. You two are the most unutterable cads and bounders I have ever met.

DAVID (*academically*). There's a great distinction between a cad and a bounder, Bertie. You shouldn't muddle the two. A cad, however low he sinks, is always a gentleman. He speaks with an Oxford accent, he has been to a public school, but a bounder is never anything but a bounder, however hard the bounder tries to be a cad, he can never get over this initial barrier. To illustrate the distinction –

TONY. A cad drinks his bathwater, but the bounder doesn't have a bath at all.

DAVID. Exactly. I could hardly have expressed it better myself. But to carry the distinction further, one might say that the cad doesn't do right by another man's wife, but the bounder doesn't do right by his own.

BERTIE. I suppose you think you're very funny, well, I think you're silly. (*Goes over to the window and looks out.*) Oh, look, there's Joan Taylor coming down the street. (*Excited.*) Perhaps she's coming in to see us.

DAVID / TONY (*together*). I hope not.

BERTIE. Yes, she is, she's at the door.

A bell is heard.

DAVID. I don't think I could bear her as early as this.

TONY. Nor could I.

DAVID. You entertain her, Bertie, will you? We're going upstairs.

TONY. We meant to do some work this morning.

DAVID. Get rid of her, Bertie, as soon as you can. When she's gone, send James up to us.

They rush out. BERTIE *straightens his tie and pats his hair. There is a knock at the door.*

BERTIE. Oh, come in, do.

Enter JAMES.

JAMES. A lady to see Mr Lister, sir.

BERTIE. Show her in, James. I'll see her.

JAMES shows her in and goes out.

Good morning, Miss Taylor.

JOAN. Oh, hello, Bertie. (*Looking round.*) Isn't David here?

BERTIE. No – he's – er, just gone out this minute.

JOAN (*disappointed*). Oh! (*After a pause; hopefully.*) Is Tony in?

BERTIE. No, I'm afraid he went out with him.

JOAN. What a pity. (*Rather tactlessly.*) Well, anyway, I've found you.

BERTIE (*awkwardly*). Yes, I'm always in in the morning. Except when I have to go to a lecture or a tutorial.

JOAN. What's a tutorial?

BERTIE. Oh, it's just a sort of interview with one's tutor. I mean – one goes to him once a week to read him one's essay.

JOAN. Oh, does he beat you if you do a bad job?

BERTIE. Oh, no.

JOAN. I suppose you never do a bad one.

BERTIE. Oh, I don't know.

JOAN. I hear you're awfully brainy.

BERTIE. Oh, really. Who told you that?

JOAN. David did. He said you were almost certain to get a fourth in your exams.

BERTIE. What! The dirty swine!

JOAN. Why? Isn't a fourth the best thing you can get?

BERTIE. No, it's the worst, except for a plough.

JOAN. Oh! (*Covering up her mistake*.) Well, anyway, I'm sure you're much cleverer than David or Tony.

BERTIE. Oh! I don't know. They're quite clever too, you know.

Pause.

JOAN. Aren't you glad the show's over? You must have had an awful lot to do as Front of House Manager. (*Invites him, by a gesture, to take a seat by her side.*)

He does so rather awkwardly, sitting on the edge of the sofa.

BERTIE. Yes, I suppose I am, really.

JOAN. It must have been an awfully difficult job – I mean, getting all those people in their right seats and everything.

BERTIE. Oh, I don't know. It's not so hard, really, when you've had some experience. Of course, I'm not saying it's easy.

JOAN. Well, I think you must be frightfully clever to have done it so well.

BERTIE. Oh, I don't know.

An awkward pause.

Can I get you a drink or something?

JOAN. No, I don't drink as a rule, thanks.

BERTIE. Of course you don't. I forgot. I think that's very wise of you.

JOAN. Well, I always say that the world would be a much better place without drink. I mean – the working classes especially –

BERTIE (*seizing the opportunity*). Work is the curse of the drinking classes.

JOAN (*bursting into shrill peals of laughter*). I say, that's awfully clever of you. Did you make that up yourself?

BERTIE. Yes, I did, as a matter of fact.

JOAN. You're a humorist, Bertie. Do you often say things like that?

BERTIE. They come to me sometimes, you know.

Pause.

Lovely day, isn't it?

JOAN. Yes, lovely.

BERTIE. Glorious.

Pause.

I hope it goes on.

JOAN. What?

BERTIE. The good weather.

JOAN. Yes.

Pause.

BERTIE. Terrible thing this Irish business.

JOAN. Is it?

BERTIE. Yes, isn't it?

Pause.

JOAN (*together*). Do you –

BERTIE (*together*). Are you –

JOAN (*together*). I'm so sorry. What were you saying?

BERTIE (*together*). I'm so sorry, what did you say?

JOAN. I was only going to say, are you very fond of the stage?

BERTIE. Yes, I am, frightfully.

Pause.

JOAN. What were you going to say?

BERTIE. I was going to ask, do you like acting?

JOAN. Yes, I do – awfully.

JOAN's knee creeps towards BERTIE's and touches it. BERTIE draws his away.

BERTIE. I'm so sorry.

JOAN. I think I ought to be going, it's getting late.

BERTIE. I say – would you like to come and have some lunch with me at the Club?

JOAN. Bertie, I'd love to.

BERTIE. That's splendid. Let us go now, shall we? We might meet some of the chaps.

JOAN (*getting up from the sofa*). All right, Bertie.

BERTIE. Before we go, do you mind – there's a telephone call I have to make – it's rather important – business, you know –

JOAN. Oh, don't mind me. (*Sits down again.*)

BERTIE (*dials a number; into phone*). Hullo! Is this Mr Blake's office? This is A.F. Arnold speaking. I want – er – half a crown each way this afternoon on Cissy, please. I said Cissy… well, there's no need to be rude, anyway. (*Puts phone down.*)

JOAN (*rising and going off with him*). I suppose you're no end of a gambler?

BERTIE. Oh, I don't know; but I do like my fun every now and then.

JOAN. What do you do on Sundays?

Exeunt JOAN *and* BERTIE. *The stage is empty for a second, then enter* PHILIP. *He looks round, goes to door and calls.*

PHILIP. James!

JAMES (*off*). Yes, sir?

PHILIP. Do you know where Mr Lister and Mr Wodehouse are?

JAMES (*off*). They are just coming downstairs, sir.

TONY and DAVID come in.

TONY. Well, what did the garage man say?

PHILIP. He said he thought it was all right.

TONY. Then have you backed Star of Africa?

PHILIP. Yes, I rang Blake up and put one hundred pounds on at sixty-six to one. He seemed very pleased.

TONY. And what have you done about the other part of the scheme?

PHILIP. I've phoned up a chap I know in London – name of Carter – he's seeing to that.

DAVID. Then there seems nothing left to do but to collect the money.

TONY. I think it's grand.

TONY and DAVID go to their respective bookcases, take down a few books each, and go to the table.

PHILIP. Are you going to work?

DAVID. Yes, for about an hour.

PHILIP. I won't disturb you. See you at lunchtime.

TONY. I won't be in to lunch.

PHILIP. Will you, David?

DAVID. Yes, I'll be in.

PHILIP. I'll be seeing you.

Exit PHILIP.

DAVID. Who you lunching with, Tony?

TONY. Who do you think?

DAVID. Not that old trout, Margot Gresham, again?

TONY. We can't be thinking of the same person. I am giving lunch to one of the great beauties of our time. Lovely Margot Gresham – glamorous, beautiful, exotic.

DAVID. Lousy.

TONY. Well, you can't talk. You'd be happy with a cow if it had the right shape.

DAVID (*pompously at first*). If you are alluding, sir, to Miss Joan Taylor – you're perfectly right.

TONY. Do you see much of her nowadays?

DAVID. Not in the daytime if I can help it. Anyway, she will be going away today now that the show's over.

TONY. Then I suppose it was to say goodbye that she came in this morning?

DAVID. Well, I'll ask her up for a weekend some time. What about Margot Gresham? Is she going away today too?

TONY. Yes, after lunch. It's our last lunch together, you know.

DAVID (*remains silent. Opens the books*). Let's start work, anyway.

TONY. Do you mind if I do a phone call before we start work? (*Picks up telephone and dials number; into phone.*) Hullo! Is that The King's Head. I want to book a table for lunch... Yes, for two. Are there any flowers on the table?... What kind... Oh! Could you get me some white roses instead, please? I'll pay for them when I come round... Wodehouse is the name. Thank you. (*Puts down the receiver.*)

DAVID (*casually*). Aren't you talking all this rather seriously, Tony?

TONY. It's got nothing to do with you.

DAVID. Well, what with sending her flowers every day and taking her to lunch and dinner, and giving parties for her, she must have cost you a good deal.

TONY (*on the defensive*). What if she has?

DAVID. Oh, I know it's none of my business – or I suppose it is, in a way.

TONY. What do you mean?

DAVID. How much money exactly do you owe me?

TONY. I don't know. I've got it written down somewhere. (*Antagonised*.) Of course, if you want it back at once –

DAVID. Don't be a fool, Tony; you can pay me back when you like.

TONY. Then, what are you getting at?

DAVID. Nothing. Only it seems so senseless squandering money on a woman who probably doesn't appreciate it, anyway.

TONY. What makes you think she doesn't appreciate it?

DAVID. A woman like that has thousands of admirers, she's not a Joan Taylor who'd fall in love with any man who gave her champagne and white roses. I don't want to be unkind, Tony, and I know you're in love with this blasted woman, but can't you make love to her in a way that wouldn't completely ruin you, as well as your bookmaker and me.

TONY (*gloomily*). Well, it'll be all over after today, anyway; she's going away and I shall probably never see her again.

DAVID. By the way, she isn't in love with you, is she?

No answer.

Do you kiss her?

Slight pause.

TONY. Yes.

DAVID. Anything else?

TONY. No.

DAVID. You don't mean to say you still regard her as the pure white goddess after all this time?

TONY. As a matter of fact, I don't feel at all the same about her as I did when I spoke to you a fortnight ago.

DAVID. Has the infatuation burgeoned into love?

TONY. Put it that way if you like.

DAVID. I hope I never fall in love. It seems to make people lose all sense of humour.

TONY. There are different kinds of love, David.

DAVID. Ah! I see. The goddess has become a woman?

TONY. Yes.

DAVID. You mean you don't want to worship her any more; you want her physically.

TONY. I want her every way.

DAVID. I see. (*Pause.*) Tony, I hope to God she doesn't fall in love with you.

TONY. Why?

DAVID. Because I don't think you're really in love with her, and as soon as you get what you want, you'll be finished with her.

TONY. But this is different.

DAVID. Oh, well, I may be wrong; anyway, she wouldn't fall in love with an overdressed little pimp like you.

TONY. Who's an overdressed pimp?

DAVID. You are. Let's do some work.

TONY. I don't feel like work.

DAVID. Do you also realise that we have three weeks to go before our final exams.

TONY. Lord, is that all?

DAVID. Do you realise that during the last two weeks, when you have been slobbering over the woman Gresham, we have done no work at all?

TONY. Yes, I'm sorry. Let's start now.

They start to work. TONY *takes a paper and pen and prepares to make notes.*

DAVID (*reads out*). 'Statutory penalties.' Crepps versus Durden. It was very wrong, of course, of Peter Crepps to be selling hot rolls on a Sunday morning instead of being at church, as it could not well be called a work of necessity and charity; it was, no doubt, a violation of the Act of Charles II of pious memory. But the Act provides for a fine of five shillings only, to be inflicted on the offender.

A bell is heard.

And therefore that worthy Magistrate at Westminster, Mr Durden, had no business whatever to say that because Crepps had sold four rolls he should be fined a pound, that is five shillings a roll.'

Enter JAMES.

JAMES (*to* TONY). Miss Margot Gresham to see you, sir.

DAVID. Blast the woman!

Throwing down his book in disgust, he rises from the table.

TONY (*pleased but apologetic*). Show her in, will you, James.

Enter MARGOT GRESHAM, *beautifully dressed.*

Hullo, Margot!

MARGOT. I've just come over to say goodbye. I hope I'm not disturbing you.

DAVID (*sarcastic*). Oh, no. We're only working.

MARGOT. Then that's all right. (*Sits down.*) And what were you working at?

DAVID. The law of torts.

MARGOT. Torts? Whatever does that mean?

DAVID (*pleasantly*). I'll give you an example. You see, if I tell Tony to beware of you because you're a menace to the youth of the nation, then you could sue me for slander. That's a tort.

MARGOT. But I couldn't if it was true, could I?

DAVID. No, you couldn't if it were true. But no court would believe it were true. You know what juries are where a pretty woman is concerned.

MARGOT. Perhaps that jury wouldn't think me pretty.

TONY. Any jury would.

MARGOT. How nice of you.

Pause.

TONY (*tactfully*). Let's have a drink.

DAVID. There's no drink in the house, I'm afraid. You had the last drop of sherry last night, Tony.

MARGOT. What a pity. I'm dying for a drink.

DAVID. There's a pub just round the corner.

MARGOT. Is there really! (*Very sweetly.*) Couldn't somebody go there and bring something here?

DAVID (*furious*). Oh, all right, if you must tope in the morning.

DAVID *goes out rather sheepishly.*

MARGOT. Now there's a boy with delightful manners. Why does he dislike me so much?

TONY. I don't know. But what does it matter? (*Kisses her.*) I wish you weren't going away this afternoon.

MARGOT. I wish I weren't too.

TONY. In all my life I've never had a happier two weeks.

MARGOT. Yes, it has been lovely.

TONY. Oh, I can't bear you going away like this. I don't know what I'll do when you've gone.

MARGOT. You'll go on living in just the same way as you used to before you ever met me. After two or three days you'll forget all about me.

TONY. That isn't true. I've kept on telling you it isn't true. I shall never forget about you as long as I live, I shall always go on loving you. Oh, Margot, can't we go away together?

MARGOT. No, Tony, no.

TONY. But why not?

MARGOT. We can't possibly, Tony. I've told you that before. You've got your exams, and I've got my work –

TONY. You're just making excuses. What's the real reason? Is it because you don't love me?

MARGOT. No, Tony; it's because I do love you.

TONY. I don't understand.

MARGOT. If you asked me to go away with you when we first met, I think I would have gone.

TONY. Then why not now?

MARGOT. Because I was only terribly attracted by you then; I wasn't in love with you.

TONY. I still don't understand.

MARGOT. I don't understand it myself. I only know that now I am in love with you, and I'm horribly frightened.

TONY. Margot, what of?

MARGOT. Of being hurt.

TONY. How could you be hurt? I wouldn't hurt you.

MARGOT. I'm not so sure, Tony. To you, the whole thing's so simple. We love each other, so why shouldn't we go away together.

TONY. Exactly.

MARGOT. Well, it's not so simple. We love each other, I know, but so differently.

TONY. What do you mean?

MARGOT. I'm so very much more in love with you than you are with me.

TONY. That's not true, Margot; I do love you passionately.

MARGOT. That's just it, and it may only be passion.

TONY. No, no, Margot; it's more than that.

MARGOT. You may think it's more, Tony, but at your age you can't really be sure.

TONY. That's nonsense.

MARGOT. It isn't. You have so many interests, so many friendships, so many exciting things in your life. Loving me is just one of them. But loving you is not just a part of my life, it's all my life. There have been other men, but this is so utterly, utterly different. Oh, I've tried so hard not to make a fool of myself like this, but I can't help it. I love you, Tony, I love you.

TONY. I'm so happy.

MARGOT. So am I, Tony. But this must be the end.

TONY. Why? Margot, if you'd come away with me –

MARGOT. Oh, don't you see, Tony? If I went away with you and we started a serious affair, it would be bound to end in disaster. If I'm to have you at all, I must have all of you, not just a part of you, the part that's in love with me. That's why it's impossible.

TONY (*sulkily*). I don't understand you.

MARGOT. Don't be angry with me, Tony. Please believe me, it would be madness to go on with this any longer. Oh, I know it'll hurt you at first, but after a bit you'll fall in love with someone else and all you'll remember of me is that we once had a lovely fortnight together.

TONY. All right, Margot. You've talked a lot of rot, and now you've got to listen to me. You're coming away with me because we're in love with each other, because we'll always be in love with each other, and because I shall never love anyone else as long as I live.

MARGOT. That's what you say now, but it's not true.

TONY. Of course it's true. All these silly excuses you've given me don't mean anything really.

MARGOT. They do, Tony, they do.

TONY. We'll be wonderfully, ecstatically happy together. This is our chance, Margot, it would be criminal to miss it.

MARGOT. Sweet, I don't want to miss it, but –

TONY. You're coming away with me, now.

MARGOT. No, Tony, no.

TONY. Yes, you are. I love you, Margot; I love you.

They kiss.

MARGOT. You're sweeping me off my feet.

TONY. Let's go now.

MARGOT. It's madness, Tony.

TONY. Then let's be mad. What does it matter?

MARGOT. But it does matter.

TONY. You're coming away with me.

MARGOT. Oh, Tony. I can't fight you any longer.

TONY. Darling!

MARGOT (*change of tone*). What about David?

TONY. David?

MARGOT. He'll be furious.

TONY. Oh, to hell with David.

Enter DAVID. *He is carrying a bottle of sherry.*

MARGOT (*looking at her watch*). Heavens, it's late! If we're going away, Tony, you had better hurry.

Exit MARGOT.

DAVID. Hi! You've forgotten your drink.

MARGOT (*off*). Haven't time.

Exit TONY.

DAVID (*shouting at* TONY). What did she mean about going away?

TONY (*going into the bedroom*). I'm going away with her for the weekend.

DAVID *follows him to the door and almost collides with him coming back, with a suitcase in his hand. The following scene must be played as fast as possible:*

DAVID. What the hell are you talking about?

TONY. I'm talking about going away with her for the weekend. (*Goes over to the bookcase.*)

DAVID (*following him round the room*). You're crazy. What about your work?

TONY. I'm taking some books with me.

TONY *takes down a couple of books and throws them into the case and rushes off into the bedroom, with* DAVID *after him.*

DAVID. Lot of use they'll be; you won't even look at them.

TONY *comes out of bedroom with clothes and throws them into the suitcase.*

TONY. Won't I? Who cares, anyway? I've been waiting for this thing to happen all my life. The most beautiful woman in the world is going away with me, and all you can do is talk of work.

At this moment he finds there is no more room in the suitcase; he picks out the books and throws them in a corner. Goes off to the bedroom again, talking all the time. DAVID *is following him about helplessly but cannot get a word in.*

(*Off.*) The trouble with you is that you don't know what love means. You're too damned materialistic. (*Comes out of the bedroom, waving a sponge.*) You've had so many lousy affairs in your life, you don't know the real thing when you see it. I'm taking your sponge. (*Throws the sponge into the suitcase.*) You and your Joan Taylors. (*Stops for breath.*)

DAVID. What are you going to use for money?

TONY. Money! What does money matter, anyway. You can lend me the money. (*Closes the suitcase, picks up his hat.*)

DAVID. But you can't go off like that, you haven't got permission.

TONY (*turns round in the doorway*). You can do that for me. Think up a story. My aunt's dead – my grandmother's dead – my sister's had triplets – anything you like. See you Monday.

Exit TONY, *slamming the door.*

DAVID (*shouting after him*). I'm damned if I will. You bloody fool!

He stands for a moment, helpless, then goes over to the corner, picks up the books which TONY *has thrown there, carries them, looking sadly at one of them, over to the table. He sits down and slowly turns over the pages. For a few moments he sits looking at the open book with his head in his hands. Slowly he reaches for the telephone, lifts the receiver and puts it on the table. With one hand still holding his head, he dials automatically for a number. He picks the receiver up.*

(*Listless voice, into phone.*) Hullo! Will you put me through to the Dean, please. (*Pause.*) Hullo, this is Lister speaking. Good morning, sir... I'm speaking for Mr Wodehouse. He was called away this morning at a moment's notice and hadn't time to see you himself. He may be away for two or three days; apparently both his aunt and his grandmother have just died... Yes, sir, very tragic indeed! However, I believe his sister is expecting a very happy event.

Scene Two

Same as in previous scene. A fortnight has elapsed. It is Derby Day.

When the curtain rises, DAVID *and* BERTIE *are discovered lunching together. They are just finishing.*

DAVID. What are you going to do this afternoon, Bertie?

BERTIE. Playing cricket, of course.

DAVID. Why, 'of course'?

BERTIE. It's the obvious thing to do on an afternoon like this.

DAVID. I can imagine a lot of things to do. Listen in to the Derby broadcast, for one.

BERTIE. Oh, is the Derby today?

DAVID (*appalled*). Bertie, please don't say things like that.

BERTIE. Why, isn't it today?

DAVID. Of course it's today. Is it possible that you didn't know it was today?

BERTIE. No, I didn't, as a matter of fact.

DAVID. Bertie, you pain me more than I can say. This is a terrible confession you are making.

BERTIE (*airily*). Oh, I don't take much interest in horse racing. The Derby means nothing to me.

DAVID. But we've been talking about nothing else in this house during the last two weeks.

BERTIE. I've got something better to do than to talk about horses.

DAVID. What?

BERTIE. Oh, work and cricket.

DAVID. Presumably you more or less have to work, but tell me seriously, Bertie, do you play cricket for enjoyment?

BERTIE. Of course.

DAVID. What do you enjoy specially about it?

BERTIE. Betting, I suppose.

DAVID. Then your enjoyment must be limited to a very short period every afternoon.

BERTIE (*offended*). As a matter of fact, I've made quite a lot of runs this season. Anyway, I don't only play cricket for the pleasure I get out of it.

DAVID. Does it give you a masochistic thrill, or something?

BERTIE. I play cricket because I think one ought to pull one's weight in one's college.

DAVID. Aren't you mixing your metaphors rather?

BERTIE. I don't mind saying that you and Tony are getting rather unpopular in college because you won't play games.

DAVID. 'Won't play games'? Squash – golf – tennis... What more do you want?

BERTIE. Those aren't games. They're not team games.

DAVID. My dear Bertie, Tony and I don't play games to improve our souls, much as they need improving. I don't like team spirit, anyway.

BERTIE. Well, it's no good arguing. I'd better get ready. (*Gets up.*)

DAVID (*looking at his watch*). I'd better be going too. Joan's train arrives in a few moments.

BERTIE (*swinging round*). Do you mean Joan Taylor?

DAVID. Yes.

BERTIE. What's she coming down here for?

DAVID. Because I want her to.

BERTIE. Why?

DAVID. I need female companionship. Besides, I like her figure.

BERTIE (*heated*). Have you brought her down here to make love to her?

DAVID. I haven't brought her down here to discuss the political situation.

BERTIE (*controlling his fury*). Have you no sense of decency at all?

DAVID. What have I done?

BERTIE. Thank God that, at any rate, in Miss Taylor you have bitten off more than you can chew.

DAVID (*with dignity*). There's no need to be obscene, Bert.

BERTIE. I warn you that, if I get a chance, I shall do all I can to stop you from ruining this little girl.

DAVID. Why don't you go and meet her at the station? Then you can explain to her how she can keep her honour in the face of my foul attacks.

BERTIE. All right, I will.

DAVID. What about your cricket?

BERTIE. I can cut that.

DAVID. Well, if you really want to go and meet her, you'd better hurry. Her train arrives in a few minutes.

BERTIE (*going to the door*). I'll take a taxi.

DAVID. You know what to do, Bertie? Slip a dagger into her hand and say... 'In the last extremity, use this!'

BERTIE. Don't be so absurd!

Exit BERTIE. *Enter* JAMES *with coffee*.

JAMES. Is Mr Arnold coming back, sir?

DAVID. He's gone to the station to meet Miss Taylor. He won't need any coffee.

JAMES. Very good, sir.

DAVID. Are you backing anything in the Derby this afternoon, James?

JAMES. Well, sir, I thought I might have a bit on the favourite, perhaps.

DAVID. Don't. Back Star of Africa.

JAMES. Star of Africa, sir?

DAVID. Yes. We've all got a fortune on it.

JAMES. Well, I hope it wins for your sake, sir, but I think I'll stick to the favourite.

Enter PHILIP.

PHILIP (*meeting* JAMES *with coffee*). Is this anyone's?

DAVID. No. Go ahead.

PHILIP *takes the coffee.* JAMES *exits.*

PHILIP. Been lunching alone?

DAVID. No. Bertie's been having lunch with me.

PHILIP. I've just met him tearing down the street in a taxi.

DAVID. Yes. I sent him to the station to meet Joan Taylor.

PHILIP. You're having her up again, are you?

DAVID. Yes, just for the night.

PHILIP. Where's Tony?

DAVID. Haven't you heard? He's gone off with that Gresham woman again.

PHILIP. What – again?

DAVID. Yes. This is the third time he's gone off with her in the last two weeks.

PHILIP. When is he coming back?

DAVID. I suppose tomorrow some time. It generally takes three days for him to recover.

PHILIP. Then he won't be here this afternoon to listen to the Derby?

DAVID. I should think he's forgotten all about the Derby by now.

PHILIP. I don't think he can fail to remember that we stand to win sixteen hundred pounds if Star of Africa wins, and a hundred pounds if it loses.

DAVID. I suppose your man in London has managed to lay off our bets all right? (*Rings for* JAMES.)

PHILIP. I haven't heard from him, but I'm sure he's managed; he would have let me know by now if he hadn't.

DAVID. Well, I hope he has. If he hasn't, we stand to lose a hundred pounds if the horse loses.

PHILIP. And we would stand to win six thousand six hundred if it wins. Still, I'm sure there's no chance of his not having laid it off.

Enter JAMES.

DAVID. You can clear now, James. (*To* PHILIP.) Do you think Star of Africa has got a real chance of winning this afternoon?

PHILIP. Lord, yes; it's a grand little horse, best bet in the race.

DAVID. What are you doing about a wireless set?

PHILIP. I'm hiring one for the afternoon. I've asked quite a lot of people in to listen. Do you mind?

DAVID. I think as Joan's coming we'd better have it in your room. Do you mind?

PHILIP. Of course not. (*Looking at his watch.*) I'll go and fetch that wireless now. Will you come with me? Oh, you've got to wait for Joan, haven't you?

DAVID. Bertie will look after her. I'll come with you. It's only just around the corner, isn't it?

PHILIP. Yes.

Exeunt DAVID *and* PHILIP. JAMES *on the stage, clearing away. He continues to clear away for a few seconds, then goes to the telephone and dials a number.*

JAMES (*into phone*). Hullo! Hullo! Is that P. Blake's office? This is J. Horton speaking. Can I speak to the boss himself, miss?... Hullo, Phil, is that you? It's Jim speaking. What's going to win this afternoon, Phil?... Oh, you think so, do you? Well, do you know what I fancy?... Star of Africa. What? You've laid it to a packet? Well, it's a grand little horse, best bet in the race... Put five bob on for me... Yes, each way. That won't break you. Goodbye.

He hears the sound of voices in the hall, puts the receiver down hurriedly and goes back to his tray.

JOAN (*off*). Don't be soft, Bertie. You are a humorist, aren't you?

JOAN *bounces in with* BERTIE *behind.*

There! I said David wouldn't be here. (*Sits on settee.*)

Exit JAMES.

BERTIE. He must have gone out for a moment. I expect he will be back. Don't worry about him.

JOAN. I'm not worrying about him, still I think he might have been here to – er – receive me.

After an awkward pause, BERTIE *sits down beside her.*

BERTIE. Joan, may I call you Joan? You call me Bertie, you know?

JOAN. Why, of course, Bertie.

BERTIE. There's a question I've been wanting to ask you for a long time. It's been worrying me dreadfully. I know it's none of my business, and you'll probably be very angry with me. Joan – (*Very intensely.*) have you ever let David – (*Pause.*) er – kiss you?

JOAN (*with a great sigh of relief*). Yes, Bertie. I'm afraid I have.

BERTIE. Oh my God, then it's worse than I thought!

JOAN. I don't understand, Bertie.

BERTIE. Of course you don't understand. (*With emotion.*)
You're so young – how could you understand?

JOAN. Bertie, is there anything wrong?

BERTIE. It's so difficult to explain these things to an innocent
little girl like you.

JOAN. Explain what?

BERTIE (*intensely*). Joan, you're in terrible danger.

JOAN (*mock alarm*). Good heavens!

BERTIE. You must leave at once before it's too late.

JOAN. But I've only just come.

BERTIE. Do you realise why you've come?

JOAN. Because David asked me.

BERTIE. And do you know why he asked you?

JOAN. Because he likes me, I suppose.

BERTIE (*brokenly*). My poor child, do you know what he wants
to do to you?

JOAN. No, Bertie.

BERTIE. He wants to – he wants to – Joan, have you ever lived
on a farm?

JOAN. No, Bertie.

BERTIE. But you know what I mean?

JOAN. Yes, Bertie.

BERTIE. Thank God! So you see, Joan, you must go at once.

JOAN. But I don't believe that of David. He's a gentleman.

BERTIE. Joan, David is a friend of mine, and it hurts me
terribly to say this about him, but where women are
concerned, he's a cad.

JOAN. I don't believe it.

BERTIE. You must believe it. He is heartless and cruel. He will treat you as he's treated scores of other girls.

JOAN. Bertie, I'm sure you're wrong.

BERTIE. I wish to Heaven I was. Go now, Joan, before you're made to realise your tragic mistake.

JOAN. I'm not going, Bertie. I trust David.

BERTIE. Well, if you're determined to stay, I warn you I shall try not to let you out of my sight for a minute.

Enter DAVID.

DAVID. Hullo, Joan. (*Gaily.*) So nice to see you. Has Bertie taken good care of you?

JOAN. Yes, thanks. He's been so kind.

DAVID. I hope you didn't mind my not being here when you arrived, but I've been helping Philip get a wireless set. He's having a lot of people in to listen to the Derby broadcast. Oh, Bertie, I wonder if you would go next door and help Philip arrange his room? I know he needs help.

BERTIE (*reluctantly*). Oh, all right. Good – bye, Miss Taylor. (*With great meaning.*) I've so enjoyed our little talk.

Exit BERTIE.

DAVID (*teasing*). So you've had a little talk, have you? I hope you haven't made any improper suggestions to him? He's not that sort of a boy, you know.

JOAN (*offended*). I don't think that's very funny, David.

DAVID (*surprised, softens*). Sorry, Joan. I didn't mean anything. (*Comes over to kiss her.*)

JOAN. I know, David, that you're so unkind to me sometimes. (*Turns her face away.*)

DAVID. Come on, Joan, don't be unfriendly. You know I don't mean to be unkind to you.

JOAN (*plaintively*). Why didn't you meet me at the station?

DAVID. As a matter of fact, I couldn't. I couldn't get away. Surely you weren't offended at that?

JOAN. And then when I arrived you weren't even here to receive me.

DAVID. Oh, come on. (*Takes her in his arms and kisses her passionately.*)

JOAN *gives way.*

JOAN (*emerging from the embrace*). Oh, David darling! You're so attractive.

DAVID. Then I'm forgiven?

JOAN *kisses him for an answer. Enter* TONY. *He carries a hat and suitcase.* JOAN *and* DAVID *break away.*

TONY (*with mock fury*). My God! Can't I get away from this sort of thing!

DAVID. I didn't expect to see you, Tony.

TONY. So it seems. Do you know, David – (*Fooling.*) the thought that buoyed me up during the darkest hours of these last terrible days...

DAVID (*in the same vein*). No, old friend. What could it be?

TONY. The thought of this cosy little nook, and our happy little circle, you at your books and Bertie addressing his envelopes and Philip deep in his *Sporting Life* by the fireside.

DAVID (*in a Noël Coward voice*). That's sweet of you, Tony, and rather touching in a quaint sort of a way.

TONY (*melodramatic*). Yes, and what do I find – sex – sex rearing its ugly head and defiling this little sanctuary of ours.

DAVID / TONY (*together, in strong Noël Coward tone*). Which we all love so much.

JOAN. I think you're a couple of lunatics.

TONY (*with emotion*). And that it should be you, Joan – you whom I have always pictured as the unplucked rose of matronly honour, that you should stand there shining in the face of God with my best friend. Have you no shame, woman!

JOAN. I think you've gone quite mad. I'm going to find Bertie. At any rate, he's sane.

TONY (*shouting after her*). Out upon you, painted Jezebel!

Exit JOAN.

DAVID. Have a good time, Tony?

TONY (*without enthusiasm*). Marvellous.

DAVID. You don't sound very enthusiastic. Why did you come back today instead of tomorrow?

TONY. I don't know.

DAVID. What excuse did you give Margot for coming back today?

TONY. I told her I had to be back to go to a tutorial. I'm supposed to be at one now.

DAVID. How did she take that?

TONY. She came with me. She's up here now.

DAVID. You know, Tony, I feel sorry for that woman, much as I dislike her.

TONY. Why?

DAVID. Because she probably realised the truth.

TONY. Which is?

Pause.

DAVID (*deliberately*). That you've fallen out of love with her as completely as you ever fell in love with her.

TONY (*quickly*). That's not true. I'm still in love with her.

DAVID. As much as you were a fortnight ago?

TONY (*hesitating*). Well – I –

DAVID. Or as much as you were when you first met her?

TONY (*hesitating again*). I – (*Suddenly, with attempted conviction.*) Yes, I am – just as much.

DAVID. You can't deceive me, Tony, even if you try to deceive yourself.

TONY (*angrily*). But it's true.

DAVID. Don't be a fool. I know perfectly well how Margot is getting on your nerves. I've been watching her almost driving you mad during the last fortnight – you've been in a hell of a temper with everyone, you've done no work, and you've been getting drunk almost every night. That's true, isn't it?

TONY. No. Yes, I suppose so. But it's not only because of Margot –

DAVID. No, it's mostly because of yourself. You've been furious with yourself for the way your feelings have changed. You refuse even to admit that they have.

TONY (*rather hysterically*). I haven't changed, I tell you.

DAVID. Then why do you tell lies to get away from her?

TONY. You don't understand, David.

DAVID. I understand perfectly. There's only one reason that prevents you from telling Margot to go to hell, and that's because she still attracts you physically. Except for that, you have no use for her whatsoever. Now, I'm right, aren't I?

TONY (*defiantly*). No.

DAVID *shrugs his shoulders and turns away.*

Oh, yes, I suppose you are. Things have changed the last few weeks. There's no use denying it. When I first met her I didn't think of her at all in that way.

DAVID. It was her mind, you said, you admired.

TONY. And then gradually I found myself frantic about her.

DAVID. I understand.

TONY. And that day when the play was over and she was going back to London and I was afraid I would lose her for ever, I made love to her. I said things to her that I've never said to any woman before. I suppose I didn't mean them really, but I wanted her so desperately that I'd have said anything, done anything – and now it has all changed.

DAVID. What has really changed?

TONY. She's just like all the others to me now, and I'm so ashamed.

DAVID. There's no reason to be, Tony.

TONY. After all, I persuaded her.

DAVID. You're not telling me she needed any persuasion. My dear Tony, you're a fool. She wanted the affair as much as you did and she had her eyes wide open.

TONY. It's nearly driven me mad.

DAVID. What, Tony?

TONY. Oh, I hate to say it, but she's madly in love with me, and I don't know what to do. I like her – one couldn't help liking her, and I can't be away from her for more than a few days when I want her frantically again, but...

DAVID. Yes?

TONY. The dreadful scenes she makes over nothing at all. If I don't say 'good morning' in the right tone of voice, our whole day is spoilt. If I forget to light her cigarette, she accuses me of not loving her any more, and she's so absurdly jealous.

DAVID. Jealous? Of whom?

TONY. It's laughable really, but she's jealous of you. She says you have a bad influence on me and that I oughtn't to see so much of you.

DAVID. How interesting. And what do you say then?

TONY. Oh, I just get angry and we scream at each other. And
then – we make it up – and then – Oh, David, what am I
going to do? She hates you for some reason or other.

DAVID. I'm not particularly fond of her, either.

TONY. Is it because of me?

DAVID. Because of you? Yes, I suppose it is.

TONY. But that's absurd, David.

DAVID. No, it isn't. That woman's created nothing but havoc
ever since she came into this house. She's interfered with our
work – she's – she's making a mess of your life. Tony, are
you going on with this affair after you've gone down?

TONY. Well, I suppose I shall go on seeing her occasionally – I
shall want to.

DAVID. Do you think that will satisfy her? She'll probably
want you to live with her, and you'll be known all over
London as Margot Gresham's lover.

TONY. Oh, no!

DAVID. But if it's only the physical side of her you want – it
must end sooner or later; why not sooner?

TONY. I could never tell her.

DAVID. I can.

TONY. Oh, no – you mustn't.

DAVID. Why not?

TONY. She'd misunderstand your motives. She…

DAVID. Has she said anything about us?

TONY. In what way?

DAVID. You know perfectly well what I mean.

TONY. Don't be absurd. She doesn't like you, that's all.

DAVID (*firmly*). I hope that *is* all. Now, listen, Tony – you must
fight this yourself. If you were really in love with her, I

wouldn't interfere, but you're not in love with her, and you'd better tell her so, and end it.

TONY. Yes, I suppose you're right.

DAVID. I know I'm right.

There is a ring.

TONY. That's her now.

He goes over to the cabinet and pours himself a stiff whisky and soda.

Enter MARGOT. *As the door opens, a hum of voices is heard from next door, where the visitors are arriving.*

DAVID (*cheerily*). Hullo, Margot. It's nice to see you.

MARGOT. It's nice to see you, David. What's Joan Taylor doing up here? Did you ask her, Tony?

DAVID. No, I did.

MARGOT. But I thought...

DAVID. That she was Tony's girlfriend? She was once, but he discarded her long ago.

MARGOT. Oh, I see. And so you've adopted her, have you?

DAVID. She was a gift from Tony.

MARGOT. Does Tony usually hand on to you his discarded women?

DAVID. Great friends should share everything, don't you think?

MARGOT. What have you brought her down here for?

DAVID. Female companionship.

MARGOT. Then why aren't you with her now?

DAVID. I don't need female companionship in the daytime. Besides, she's with Bertie.

MARGOT. Do you think she enjoys being with that idiot?

DAVID. My dear, you don't know her. She's probably very happy. God knows what they talk about, but they do talk, whereas whenever I'm with her I can never find a thing to say to her.

MARGOT. If you think that, why don't you leave her to him altogether?

DAVID. I probably will when I've finished with her.

MARGOT. Some day, David, I'm going to get very angry with you.

DAVID (*innocently*). Why, what have I said?

MARGOT. Aren't you afraid that someone will hurt you as you hurt others?

DAVID. I'm not aware of hurting others.

MARGOT. You're hurting Joan, aren't you?

DAVID. Not that I'm aware of.

MARGOT. You're going to see her tonight at the hotel.

DAVID. Yes. How did you know?

MARGOT. Obviously that's what you had her up here for.

DAVID. Anyway, how can that hurt her? The only one that can get hurt is me.

MARGOT. What do you mean?

DAVID. If the Proctors caught me, I should get sent down. Still, there's not much chance of that. I'm not a damn fool.

MARGOT (*to* TONY). You're very silent, darling. What's the matter with you? Are you depressed about something?

TONY. No, Margot.

DAVID. I think he's had a bad tutorial this afternoon.

TONY. What do you mean, David. What tutorial?

DAVID (*meaningly*). The one you had this afternoon, of course.

TONY. But I haven't had… (*Covering up his confusion.*) Oh, yes – yes, it was a bad one.

MARGOT. Tony, why did you lie to me?

TONY. What do you mean, Margot?

MARGOT. You told me you had to be back this afternoon to go to a tutorial.

TONY. Margot, I –

MARGOT. That wasn't true, was it?

TONY. Oh, it wasn't altogether, but I had to be back here this afternoon, really, Margot, and I thought –

MARGOT. But why didn't you just tell me you wanted to come back? I should have understood. I hate you telling me lies, Tony.

TONY. I'm sorry.

MARGOT. What was the real reason for coming back?

TONY. There wasn't any definite reason – just that –

DAVID (*breaking in*). What you don't seem to realise, Margot, is that every day Tony spends away from the university with you, he makes his chance of a degree more hopeless.

MARGOT. I should have thought that was Tony's affair, not yours!

DAVID. What is Tony's affair, is mine.

MARGOT. Why?

DAVID. Because of our friendship.

MARGOT. 'Friendship'?

DAVID. Of course, that is hardly something I could expect you to understand.

MARGOT. I understand it better than you think. I'm not altogether blind.

DAVID. Aren't you?

MARGOT. You think I don't see through all this clever talk.

DAVID. No, I didn't mean that.

MARGOT. Well, I do see through it. What I've said to Tony about you, I'll say to you now. I've told him that you had a bad influence on him with your filthy ideas of women and sex...

TONY (*interfering*). Don't, Margot, please.

MARGOT. Leave me alone. (*To* DAVID.) You're incapable of appreciating anything that isn't your own level. You think that I gave myself to Tony for the same reason that Joan gives herself to you.

DAVID. What else would you expect me to think?

MARGOT. With your depraved mentality, nothing else. You could look on me as another of the women in Tony's life. You couldn't realise that he might really be in love with me, and that I might really be in love with him, because love is something that is utterly beyond you. Well, he is in love with me, and I am in love with him, and nothing that you or anyone in the world can do will separate us. Tony – that's true, isn't it?

Enter BERTIE *and* JOAN.

DAVID. Hullo, Joan. Has Bertie been amusing you?

JOAN. He's been keeping me in fits; he said such a clever thing to me just now. Do tell them what you said, Bertie.

DAVID. Yes, do, Bertie.

BERTIE *hesitates*.

BERTIE. Oh, well, I only said it is better to be good-looking than good.

All remain silent except JOAN, *who is overcome with laughter.*

TONY (*very slightly drunk*). You'll slay me with your cracks, Bertie.

JOAN. Do let's all go next door, there's such a lovely party going on.

They all signify their assent and move towards the door, except TONY, *who remains where he is. As* MARGOT *is about to go out of the door,* TONY *calls to her.*

TONY. Don't go in there for a moment, Margot.

MARGOT. Darling, don't be angry with me, I couldn't help it. He's got to understand. I've got to make him. Every time you are with him. I feel he is drawing you away from me. Oh, Tony, why are you so weak?

TONY. Listen to me, Margot, where is all this leading us to? You know the term ends in a fortnight and my people will expect me to go straight home.

MARGOT. Yes.

TONY. Well, surely you see –

MARGOT. Tony, what is it?

TONY. After all, we're not very happy, are we?

MARGOT. Aren't we?

TONY. The dreadful rows –

MARGOT. They don't mean anything.

TONY. They mean a lot to me.

MARGOT. I don't see what you're trying to tell me.

TONY. If we could marry, it would be different.

MARGOT. Can't we?

TONY. You know I haven't got any money.

MARGOT. I have plenty.

TONY. I couldn't live on you.

MARGOT. You could live with me.

TONY. And be known all over London as Margot Gresham's lover.

MARGOT. That's David talking, Tony, not you. I told you he'd
try and separate us, and you're letting him. I thought you'd
stand out against him. I thought you loved me enough to do
that, but now I believe that even if you did love me as much
as I love you, you'd still let David come between us.

TONY. David has nothing to do with this.

MARGOT. He has everything to do with it.

TONY. I tell you, David has nothing to do with this change.

MARGOT (*struck*). 'Change'? Oh, Tony, then you have
changed?

TONY *bows his head.*

Oh, my darling, you can't mean that? Have you forgotten the
wonderful times we've had together? Have you forgotten the
wonderful things we've said to each other? You did love me
– I know that. I wasn't just a woman in your life. I wanted to
be the only woman – you made me believe I was.

TONY. Oh, Margot.

MARGOT. Come away with me now. You do love me really.

TONY. Don't, Margot.

MARGOT. Tony, don't hurt me – you said you wouldn't –
darling, look at me –

Enter PHILIP.

PHILIP. Hullo, you two. If you want to hear the Derby you'd
better come now. The horses have gone to post.

Voices off. TONY *moves to go with* PHILIP. *Shout from next
door.*

VOICE. They're off!

PHILIP. Come on.

He turns to rush off, as JAMES *appears at the doorway with
a telegram. The door is still open and all is quiet next door,
except for the sound of a wireless talking.*

JAMES. Telegram for you, Mr Kahn.

PHILIP (*opening telegram*). I wonder who it's from? (*Reads*.) Good God!

TONY. What's the matter?

PHILIP. Listen to this: 'Unable to find backers Star of Africa twenty-two to one.'

TONY. What does that mean?

PHILIP. Don't you see, we've got to find one hundred pounds between us if it loses.

Enter BERTIE.

BERTIE. Star of Africa's leading. (*Darts back next door*.)

TONY. But if it wins, how much do we win?

PHILIP. Six thousand pounds.

TONY. Oh, God, let it win.

PHILIP. Come on – we can hear the end of the race.

TONY. I couldn't bear to listen to it.

Enter BERTIE.

BERTIE. Star of Africa's still leading at Tattenham Corner. (*Darts back next door*.)

Exit PHILIP *and* TONY. MARGOT *alone on the stage. From next door comes a sudden roar and cheers.*

VOICES (*off*). Star of Africa! Star of Africa! Star of Africa won it! Hurrah! Whoopee!

MARGOT *pulls herself together, tries to compose herself, as* JOAN, BERTIE, TONY, DAVID *and* PHILIP *come whoopee-ing into the room.*

TONY *jumps up on a chair and starts singing the refrain, which they all take up. Shouted in the form of a toast, the whole song is to the tune of 'John Brown's Body'.*

TONY (*singing*).
     We can conquer unemployment,
     We can conquer unemployment,

We can conquer unemployment,
When we get back next May.
Next May.

JAMES *puts his head in the doorway.*

JAMES. What won, sir?

DAVID *puts something very loud and hot on the gramophone.*

TONY. Star of Africa, you old bag!

JAMES. Hurrah! (*Loses his dignity completely and dances out.*)

TONY. I tell you what –

The noise subsides.

Let's all go out and buy cases of champagne. We'll have a real party.

MARGOT. Tony, stay with me.

All except DAVID and MARGOT, whoop out, led by TONY.

The gramophone continues to blare out its discord. MARGOT is standing in the middle of the room, staring abstractedly. Suddenly she becomes conscious of the gramophone. The harsh blare unnerves her. She rushes over to the gramophone and dashes the sound box off across the record. It makes a harsh grating noise.

DAVID (*swinging round on her*). What did you do that for?

MARGOT. Because I'm sick of it. Sick of you and all your crowd of screaming, brawling children. (*Takes the record off and crashes it to the floor.*)

DAVID. You're being a bit melodramatic, aren't you?

MARGOT. I suppose you think you've won?

DAVID. What do you mean?

MARGOT. You think you've got Tony away from me?

DAVID. My dear Margot…

MARGOT. Ever since you met me, you've been trying to poison Tony against me – and now you think you've won – you haven't, do you hear? Tony'll always come back to me. You may have got him now, but he'll see through you in time.

DAVID. You don't know what you're saying – Tony and I...

MARGOT. Oh, yes, I know all about Tony and you. I know the influence you've had on that boy – I know how you put him up to say what he did to me just now. It wasn't him speaking at all; it was you speaking through him. Every word he said –

DAVID. You must be mad.

MARGOT. Perhaps I am mad, but Tony is the one great thing in my life, and I won't let him go.

DAVID. How many times have you said that before?

MARGOT. Oh, I don't deny there have been other men in my life. Why should I? But with Tony it's different. He's a part of me – I'm a part of him that even you can't separate.

DAVID. Why would I want to separate you?

MARGOT. I'll tell you why – I'm not afraid of you, you can't fool me – because you're just a filthy degenerate!

DAVID. God! How dare you? You who come down here and seduce a boy half your age... You who've done your best to ruin his life for him – he's up to his neck in debt and he'll go down without a degree, and all because of you – you talk about degeneracy.

MARGOT. You –

Breathless with rage, she turns towards him, when she hears the noise of the others returning, then she runs to the door, pausing to say –

I won't forget this.

Exit MARGOT. *Enter* TONY, *followed by the others.*

TONY. Hullo, David. What's the matter?

DAVID (*very slowly, with an effort*). Is that champagne you've got, Tony?

TONY. Yes. Cordon Rouge.

DAVID (*to them all*). Let's all get roaring, screaming drunk.

The revelry begins again as the curtain comes down.

ACT THREE

Scene One

A bedroom in The King's Head Hotel. It is a large room with a double bed. Furniture in the usual style of a provincial hotel. The room is on the first floor. In the back wall is a window overlooking the yard. The bed runs from the left wall to the centre of the stage. The door is in the right wall downstage; it leads into a corridor, which is on the stage and visible to the audience. At the further end of the corridor, stairs lead down into the hall. Doors lead off from the corridor to upper rooms.

As the curtain rises, JOAN *is discovered in the bedroom. She is slightly tipsy from the celebration. She is singing to herself while undressing.*

JOAN (*singing*).
> We can conquer unemployment,
> We can conquer unemployment,
> We can conquer unemployment,
> Next May –

As she shouts this last she falls backwards onto the bed and kicks her legs in the air. When she has finished undressing, she puts on her dressing gown and settles into bed to read.

(*Into phone.*) Is that the porter? This is Miss Taylor speaking, yes, Miss Taylor. (*Little laugh.*) T – for Tommy, A – for Agnes – Oh, it doesn't matter… Will you put me on to Margot, please… what… oh, Miss Gresham… (*While waiting.*) Silly man… Oh, is that you, Margot dear… this is Joan, J – for Jewel box, O – for, Oh, look what is the matter with me? Margot, dear, do come round for a moment, I've got something I want to show you. No, the *first* floor… second door on the – (*Hiccups.*) right – (*Puts phone down.*) Tight as a lord.

Knock at the door.

Enter MARGOT.

MARGOT. Hullo, Joan.

JOAN. Why weren't you at the party? It was lovely.

MARGOT. I've got a headache.

JOAN. I'll have one in the morning, too.

MARGOT. Why, did you drink a lot?

JOAN. I don't remember, I must have. It was such a lovely party, and everyone got so gay. Whoopee! Have a sweet?

MARGOT. Thanks. Did Tony get drunk as well?

JOAN. I don't know about Tony, but David got so drunk he gave me this.

MARGOT. It's charming.

JOAN. He bought it for me this afternoon and meant to give it to me in here, but he just couldn't wait... He is sweet.

MARGOT. Are you in love with him?

JOAN. Why?

MARGOT. I suppose it doesn't really matter. Where is he now?

JOAN. He's with Tony, of course.

MARGOT. I knew it.

JOAN. Knew what?

MARGOT. Sometimes I tried to think I was wrong, tried to fool myself I was wrong, but now I know I was right. Oh God, I know I'm right.

JOAN. You're being a bit theatrical, aren't you?

MARGOT. Joan, don't you understand?

JOAN. No, darling, I don't. I think you need a good sleep.

MARGOT (*half to herself*). I'll get even with him yet. He'll be sorry he ever came between us.

JOAN. I don't know what you're talking about. I wish David would come.

MARGOT. You're sure he'll come here tonight?

JOAN (*laughing*). Oh, you are funny. Of course he will.

MARGOT. Joan, don't you think you're being rather foolish?

JOAN. Getting drunk? Yes, it's foolish, but it feels nice.

MARGOT. I didn't mean that.

JOAN is seated at the dressing table trying in a semi-drunken way to make herself up.

These boys, they can cause such havoc in our lives – if we take them seriously.

JOAN. Why take anything seriously, I don't.

MARGOT. I know. Perhaps you've no need to. I should have known better – I'm old enough to have known better. It's a difficult life for women.

JOAN. It's a grand life, I think.

MARGOT. At your age, I suppose it is. Nothing matters much when you're twenty. Somehow I think one's heart doesn't beat at twenty, it just lies waiting to get hurt like some dumb thing that must suffer without crying out.

JOAN is gradually listening.

Oh, the pain – the unending pain, that even tears will not soothe –

JOAN. Margot, dear, I hate to see you like this, on such a lovely night, after such a lovely day.

They sit on the bed together, but MARGOT *speaks to herself.*

MARGOT. If only I'd never come to this place at all. Why was I such a fool? I should have known – I should have known... David's like that, cold, heartless, it gives him pleasure to tear me to pieces.

JOAN *has risen at the mention of* DAVID, *and stands looking perplexed at* MARGOT.

JOAN. I don't understand you, Margot.

MARGOT*'s voice has become hard and desperate and rises to a pitch of excitement.*

MARGOT. I'll hurt him somehow, I'll find a way.

JOAN. Darling, you ought to go to bed. You're ill. You need a good sleep.

MARGOT (*suddenly turning on her; her voice calm again, but with sinister meaning*). Are you sure David's coming here tonight?

JOAN. Of course.

MARGOT. Then I must go.

JOAN. Yes, that's right, Margot. Go to bed. You'll be all right in the morning.

MARGOT. Goodbye, Joan. Keep your youth and enjoy it. Forgive my rambling on like this but I had to talk or I think I should have gone mad.

JOAN. I wish I could help you.

MARGOT. No one could do that but myself – and time.

A knock at the door.

JOAN. Who's there?

MARGOT (*in a whisper*). Wait a moment. (*Pulls herself together.*) All right.

JOAN. Come in.

Enter DAVID.

DAVID. Hullo, the lovely lady Margot – an unexpected pleasure.

MARGOT. Goodnight, Joan.

DAVID. I shouldn't wait up for him – he's gone to bed.

Exit MARGOT. DAVID *closes the door and jumps on the bed.*

JOAN (*playfully*). Look out for my toes, you brute!

DAVID *bounces up and down on the bed.*

David, you're tiddly!

DAVID. So are you, you old trout! I haven't met anybody who is sober tonight. Even the Proctors are drunk.

JOAN. David, you didn't run into the Proctors.

DAVID. No, but I saw them in the distance, staggering down the street playing leaping with the Bullers.

JOAN. Oh, David, you didn't. What is a Buller, David?

DAVID. A nasty little man in a bowler hat and white gloves who catches you if you run away from a Proctor.

JOAN. I don't really know what a Proctor is.

DAVID. You don't see them in the daytime. (*In a bedtime-story manner.*) They only come out at night. They wait at street corners and when they see a nice tasty little boy like me come along, they turn themselves suddenly into pillar boxes, and just as you're going to post your little letter they change back suddenly into Proctors.

JOAN. Why?

DAVID. Don't you see, he's swallowed your little letter.

JOAN. Why, what was in the letter?

DAVID. Well, that's the awful part. Nobody'll ever know.

JOAN. You are tiddly, David.

DAVID (*standing up. With great dignity*). Madame! The boot is on the other leg, I warrant. It is you who are suffering, if I may so express it, from overindulgence.

JOAN *is about to interrupt him, but he waves her aside.*

Nay, Baroness, pray do not apologise. I myself, though I blush to confess it, have at times wallowed in the pleasures of inebriation. (*Suddenly coming down to earth.*) Why, you old bag, you're so drunk you think everybody else is drunk.

He bounces on the bed again and kisses her protests away.

JOAN. David, do you behave yourself.

DAVID *falls back to the foot of the bed. He passes his hands over his eyes.*

DAVID. Gosh! I am drunk!

JOAN. Well, anyway, you did win the Derby and two thousand today.

DAVID. Yes, doesn't it seem incredible? Two thousand.

JOAN. What are you going to do with all that money, David?

DAVID. Well, it's all rather difficult. You see, my first idea was to buy two thousand little girls like you and put them all in a beautiful harem with fountains playing and enormous divans and naked statues, with lovely thick carpets just like the Empire Cinema. But then I thought, no, people would talk. No. When a thing like that gets about, it's hard to stop people talking.

JOAN. But seriously, David, what are you going to do with the money?

DAVID. Well, I'll tell you, but you must promise not to tell a soul because it's all a great secret. I'm going to put it into the Bank. (*Pause.*) Then I'm going to use it to start me on my brilliant career. I've never told you about my career, have I, Joan?

JOAN (*rather bored*). No, David.

DAVID (*sitting up*). Your interest in the subject is so obvious that I shall reward you with a brief sketch of my meteoric rise to fame. On leaving the university, with a brilliant record and, of course, first-class honours, I shall immediately become a promising young journalist. Wherever the English language is read or spoken, politicians will tremble at the name of David Lister. The rich oppressor in his marble palace, sipping his early-morning champagne in his vast, luxurious bed, starts and turns pale at the sight of the morning paper. 'Lister will be the death of us,' he creaks, and his glass untasted slips from his hand. The poor oppressed in his lowly hovel, crumpling his black bed and quenching his thirst with great gulps of cold water – (*Registers disgust.*) has spent his last earnings – a few pennies at most – in buying his evening paper. Feverishly, he turns over the pages, searching for the words that are not there. 'What, no Lister!' he cries. 'What a ruddy shame!' His little brat playing on the hearth has found a photograph. In his childish ignorance he does not know that noble face, those stern but kindly eyes. With a gesture of disgust he makes to throw it in the fire. In a single bound, his father is upon him. He snatches the photograph away. A strange tenderness lights up his features as he put the photograph to his lips; then, throwing out his hairy chest and raising his horny hand in salute, he shouts 'Hail, Lister! The people's friend! The man for the masses!'

There is a knock at the door.

Who's there?

Another knock.

Who is it?

BULLER (*through the closed door*). The Proctor's Buller, sir. Are you a member of this university?

Pause.

DAVID. Yes.

BULLER. The Senior Proctor wishes to speak to you, sir. He is waiting downstairs.

Pause.

DAVID. Do you mind waiting while I dress?

BULLER. All right, sir. Don't be long.

JOAN (*in a stage whisper*). What's the matter, David?

DAVID (*all in a whisper*). It's the Proctors. How the hell did they know I was here?

JOAN. Someone must have told them.

DAVID. Who could have told them? Nobody knows I'm here.

He is walking about desperately. Stops suddenly.

God! Margot knows I'm here. She told them. She wants to get me sent down, the dirty bitch. Well, they haven't got me yet. (*Goes over to the window and looks out.*)

JOAN. What are you going to do ?

DAVID. There's a drainpipe. I think I can do it. Anyway, it's worth a shot.

JOAN. Don't, David, you'll kill yourself.

DAVID *is already over the top and gone.*

BULLER. Are you coming, sir?

There is no reply. The BULLER *waits for a second, becomes suspicious, then turns to the* PORTER.

Open the door, will you?

The PORTER *opens the door with his skeleton key and the* BULLER *rushes in. He takes a quick look round and goes over to the window. Looks out.*

(*Shouting to his friend.*) Bill, the blighter's climbed out of the window. Run down – you can cut him off in the high street.

The PORTER *runs off.* MARGOT *appears in the passage. The* BULLER *goes out, turns at the door.*

(*To* JOAN.) Goodnight, miss. I'm sorry about your young man.

JOAN. Will he get away?

BULLER (*shaking his head, deliberately*). No, miss. He hasn't got a chance.

The BULLER *goes out.*

Curtain.

Scene Two

*The same as in Acts One and Two. The next morning, about
10:00 a.m.*

TONY *is discovered on the stage. He is sitting at the table,
having just finished breakfast. He is reading the morning paper.
He wears pyjamas and an expensive dressing gown.* JAMES
enters.

JAMES. May I clear now, sir?

TONY (*gloomily*). Yes.

JAMES (*as he is clearing*). Is it true that Mr Lister was caught
in The King's Head by the Proctors last night?

TONY. Yes, James. How did you know?

JAMES. I heard Mr Kahn talking about it this morning. Will he
be sent down, sir?

TONY. He's with the Proctors now. I don't think he's got a
chance.

JAMES. I *am* sorry, sir. It's a terrible thing to happen just at this
time, three weeks before his final schools. He would have
got a first, wouldn't he?

TONY. I expect so, James.

JAMES. But how did it happen, sir? I don't understand. The
Proctors never go there at that time of night.

TONY. Someone gave him away.

JAMES. Are you sure, sir?

TONY. Yes, quite sure.

JAMES. Do you know who it was?

TONY. Yes.

JAMES. Oh, well, if you know who it was, I suppose you and Mr Lister will know how to deal with him.

TONY (*half to himself*). Yes, we'll know how to deal with her.

JAMES. With her, sir?

TONY. Yes, with her.

JAMES. Oh. Well, please believe me, when I say that I am very very sorry.

TONY. I do, James. Thanks very much.

Exit JAMES. TONY *picks up his paper, and in a moment* PHILIP *enters. He is very excited.*

PHILIP. Have you heard the news, Tony?

TONY. No, David isn't back yet.

PHILIP. I mean about Blake.

TONY. What about Blake?

PHILIP. He welched – the dirty blackguard.

TONY. What? How do you know?

PHILIP. I've just been round to his office to see if everything was all right, and it's boarded up.

TONY. Well, that doesn't mean he's welched. He may have gone away for a holiday.

PHILIP. He's welched all right. Apparently, we weren't the only people to back Star of Africa at sixty-six to one. He's dropped a fortune on the race.

TONY. But he may have gone away to collect some money or something.

PHILIP. Not a chance. There's a crowd around his office already, and the police are there. They say he's left the country.

TONY. But he couldn't do that.

PHILIP. 'Fraid so, Tony. I'm afraid we'll have to say goodbye to our little fortune.

TONY. Isn't there any way of making him pay?

PHILIP. Not an earthly.

TONY *makes a gesture of despair.*

Cheer up, Tony. It might be worse. At least we didn't lose anything on the race.

TONY. I'm not thinking of us, I'm thinking of David. I don't know how we can break the news to him.

PHILIP. God, yes. I'd forgotten about him. Has he come back from the Proctors yet?

TONY. No.

PHILIP. You're right, Tony, it'll be hell to have to tell him. I heard him say this morning that it didn't matter so much if he was sent down, because he'd still have that two thousand he won yesterday.

TONY. Why should all this happen to us? It's so damned unfair.

PHILIP. We've just fiendish bad luck, that's all.

TONY. I think I could kill Margot.

PHILIP. You know, Tony, I feel a little sorry for her.

TONY. How can you say that after all that's happened?

PHILIP. I don't believe she can have known what she was doing last night. I know it was a lousy thing to do, but she may have had some excuse for it.

TONY (*savagely*). Is there any excuse for ruining a man's life?

Enter DAVID.

DAVID. Hey, who's talking about ruining my life?

TONY. Why, didn't they send you down?

DAVID. Of course they sent me down.

TONY. I'm sorry, David.

DAVID. Oh, well, cheer up. I'm not the first person to get sent down. Shelley was sent down, it didn't affect his career very much.

TONY. Yes, but Shelley didn't go into politics.

DAVID. Oh, I know of plenty of better occupations than politics. It ought to be quite easy to get a good job with my two thousand pounds.

TONY and PHILIP exchange glances.

Why, what's the matter?

TONY (*going to him*). David, I've got to tell you something.

DAVID. What is it, Tony?

A silence.

Well?

TONY. Blake's welched on us.

A silence.

DAVID (*very restrained*). Are you sure?

PHILIP. I've just been round to his office. He's gone all right.

DAVID (*very slowly*). How extremely funny. (*Laughs.*)

TONY (*amazed*). But, David, don't you realise what this means?

DAVID. Yes, Tony, I realise what it means, but I still think it's damned funny.

TONY. Well, I wish I could see the funny side of it. Two thousand pounds means a lot to me.

DAVID. What do you think it means to me?

TONY (*immediately sorry*). I'm sorry, David. It means more to you than to any of us, really.

PHILIP. Well, I'm going to have a strong drink. We certainly need it.

PHILIP goes to the door. TONY follows him.

Coming, David?

DAVID. No, Philip, I'm staying here.

DAVID sits for a moment, staring ahead, then tries to pull himself together, walks over to his bookcase, takes books down, looks at them to see if they are his, and puts them on the table. While he is doing this, there is a knock at the door, and, as he does not answer, JOAN comes in. He takes no notice of her.

JOAN (*timidly*). David.

DAVID (*in the same bored voice*). Hullo, Joan.

JOAN. What happened last night, David? Did they catch you?

DAVID. Yes.

JOAN. Are they going to expel you?

DAVID. Yes.

JOAN. I'm so sorry, David. I feel it's all my fault.

DAVID. Do you?

JOAN (*trying to be bright*). Well, every cloud has a silver lining. Now you don't have to do your exams, do you?

DAVID. No, Joan. I don't have to do my exams.

JOAN. And you have got two thousand pounds, haven't you?

DAVID. No, I haven't –

JOAN. Don't be soft, David. You know you won two thousand pounds yesterday.

DAVID (*turning round on her in a sudden fury*). Oh, for God's sake, Joan, go away. Can't you see I want to be left alone?

JOAN. Oh, David. (*Goes to him.*)

DAVID. Do you want me to make love to you at this time of morning, because I won't. (*Pushes her.*)

JOAN (*jumping up with a burst of temper*). Oh, you brute, you call yourself a gentleman? Bertie was right. You think you can do what you like with me, don't you? You make love to me at night, and then talk to me like this in the morning. You think I'm cheap, don't you?

DAVID. Why must all women talk about yourselves as though you were prostitutes. You're frightened of being thought cheap, aren't you? All right, then, I'll say you're expensive if you like. The most expensive girl I know. (*Flings out.*) You women make me sick. (*Exits.*)

JOAN is left crying on the sofa. She sobs her heart out. After a few seconds the door opens slowly and BERTIE's *hand appears rather nervously. Seeing* JOAN *alone, he comes in.*

BERTIE. I say, what's up, Joan? (*Comes over and sits next to her on the sofa, rather gingerly.*)

JOAN (*still crying*). Nothing, Bertie.

BERTIE. I bet David's at the bottom of this. What's he been saying to you?

JOAN. He's been so unkind to me, Bertie.

BERTIE. The cad. What did he do?

JOAN (*between sobs*). He called me dreadful names. He said I was a prostitute.

BERTIE (*getting up, indignant*). The rotten swine. He ought to be horsewhipped. God, if I could only lay my hands on him. I'd thrash him within an inch of his life.

At this moment, DAVID *walks in. He takes no notice of them, walks to the table, picks up a book and walks out.* BERTIE *rushes up to him as he is walking out, and attempts to bar his way.*

You dirty rotter. How dare you talk to Joan like that? I've a good mind to knock you down.

They are standing behind the sofa as he says this. DAVID *impatiently pushes him aside.* BERTIE *falls backwards over the sofa and lands on the floor almost at* JOAN's *feet.* DAVID *walks out.*

JOAN (*bending down to help him up, very tenderly*). You're not hurt, Bertie, are you? Oh, you poor darling.

BERTIE (*getting up fussily and brushing himself down*). He was too quick for me, the cad. For two pins I'd go after him and give him a hiding he'd never forget. (*Makes as if to go to the door.*)

JOAN *restrains him.*

JOAN. Don't go, Bertie, he'll hurt you.

BERTIE. What, he hurt me? Why, I'll break every bone in his body. I'll murder him.

JOAN. Yes, Bertie, I know you would. But I don't want you to get into any trouble for my sake. Please stay with me.

BERTIE. Well, of course, if you want me to stay, I'll stay. Still, one day I'll give him what he deserves.

JOAN. I hope you do, Bertie, it was ripping of you to stand up for me like that.

BERTIE. Oh, I don't know. Any other chap would have done the same in my place.

JOAN. Well, I think it was wonderfully brave of you. No one's ever done a thing like that for me before.

Pause.

BERTIE (*genuinely modest*). Oh, it was nothing.

JOAN. Do you know, Bertie, I think I'd like to kiss you.

BERTIE *is taken by surprise but says nothing.*

May I?

BERTIE *still says nothing. She bends forward and kisses him tenderly on the mouth.*

BERTIE (*dazed*). Do that again, please, Joan.

JOAN *does it again. This time a much longer kiss. Almost passionately.*

So you don't love David any more.

After a short pause.

JOAN. I never did love him. And now I hate him.

BERTIE. Joan, there's something I've been wanting to say for a long time, and I've never had the courage. Joan, do you think... could you... do you think you could learn to love me?

JOAN (*hesitatingly*). I've never felt like this for anyone before. It's such a lovely warm feeling. I think I've loved you all the time, really.

BERTIE. Will you marry me, Joan?

JOAN. Oh, Bertie, I couldn't.

BERTIE. Why not if you love me?

JOAN. Because I'm not worthy of you.

BERTIE. Nonsense, you're just as good as I am.

JOAN. Oh, but you must think me so wicked.

BERTIE. Rubbish. If you mean David forcing his way into your room last night, I understand perfectly. He was blind drunk or else he couldn't have done it. Thank God, the Proctors came.

JOAN. Oh, Bertie, darling. (*Throws herself into his arms.*) Now we can go and live on a farm.

They kiss. While they are kissing, the door opens and TONY *and* PHILIP *walk in very gloomily.*

PHILIP. Oh, Bertie, you've been deceiving us.

BERTIE. You may congratulate us. We're engaged to be married.

TONY. You'll slay me with your cracks.

BERTIE. But we're serious. (*Looks at* JOAN *proudly*.) Joan's promised to become Mrs Arnold.

PHILIP (*with assumed heartiness*). Say, Bertie, how perfectly topping.

TONY (*without enthusiasm*). Top hole.

PHILIP (*to* BERTIE). You must take care of the little woman,
I'm sure she'll make you a ripping little missus. You're a
lucky fellow, Bertie. You've beaten us all to it.

BERTIE. Thank you, Philip, old boy. I'll do my best to make
her a fine husband.

TONY. You'll make a fine pair.

PHILIP (*to* JOAN). So you're taking Bertie from us, are you?
Well, we'll miss him.

TONY. Yes, we're going to miss him.

PHILIP. But I for one wouldn't want to stand in the way of his
happiness.

TONY. Nor I.

JOAN. Thank you all so much. I'm not really taking Bertie
from you, because we'll come and see you every so often.

PHILIP. And you must bring the little ones along. I'm so fond
of children.

BERTIE (*deprecatingly*). I say, old chap. (*Then jocularly.*)
Remember there's a lady present. Come on, Joan. If we stay
here any longer they might say anything. Well, cheer-ho,
chaps. Got to buy the little girl a ring, you know.

BERTIE *and* JOAN *exit.*

PHILIP. Well, that's that. God moves in mysterious ways His
wonders to perform. Perhaps it's all for the best.

TONY. Do you realise those two are going to breed?

PHILIP. Well, we've got to have halfwits in the world otherwise
we'd have no one to laugh at.

Enter DAVID.

DAVID. Have they gone?

TONY. Bertie's proposed to her.

DAVID. Proposed what?

TONY. Why, marriage, of course.

DAVID. Well, good luck to both of them. They'll need it. Fancy those two having to sit opposite each other for the next forty years.

PHILIP. Perhaps they'll have breakfast in bed.

DAVID. Well, I'm pleased about it. I'm afraid I got rid of most of my fury this morning on Joan, poor girl. Still, my brutality seems to have driven her into Bertie's arms. So it was all for the best really.

TONY. But what about Margot? If she treated me the way she did you – I think I'd kill her.

DAVID. Last night after it happened, I lay awake for hours thinking out ways of getting even with her. Then gradually I began to see the situation more clearly. She didn't ring up the Proctors because she's naturally malevolent, but because she's in love with you.

TONY. I don't see what that's got to do with it.

DAVID. Well, don't you see, she thought I was trying to take you away from her, and she thought that deserved any punishment.

TONY. I think her action was unforgiveable.

PHILIP. Well, I suppose I'd better go and do some work. When are you going down, David?

DAVID. Some time this afternoon, I suppose.

PHILIP. Well, I'll see you before I go, won't I?

DAVID. Of course.

PHILIP. I'll be in this afternoon to give you a tearful send-off. So long.

DAVID. Well, if I'm going to pack, I'd better begin on these books. Tony, can you lend me something I can take them away in?

TONY. Yes, you can have that trunk of mine. I say, David, this all makes it easy now, doesn't it?

DAVID. About what?

TONY. About Margot. She'll never come back here again – it's all over.

DAVID. Yes, it's all over.

TONY. It's damned hard lines on you, though, and it's all my fault.

DAVID. Don't talk rot, Tony.

TONY. I'll get that trunk.

Exit TONY. DAVID *goes to the bookcase. Enter* JAMES.

JAMES. Miss Gresham is here, sir. She wants to see you alone.

DAVID. I am not in to Miss Gresham, James.

JAMES. Yes, sir.

TONY (*off*). Is that James?

JAMES. Yes, sir.

TONY (*off*). Give me a hand with this trunk, will you?

JAMES looks at DAVID *who nods 'yes'. Exit* JAMES.

(*Off.*) Careful, that handle's loose.

TONY *and* JAMES *enter carrying a small flat trunk, which they place by the table.*

JAMES (*to* DAVID). Shall I ask Miss Gresham to wait, sir?

TONY. Miss Gresham. (*To* DAVID.) Is Margot here?

DAVID. Yes, she wants to see me alone. I'm not seeing her.

JAMES. She seems very upset, sir.

DAVID (*giving* TONY *a bundle of books*). Start with these, Tony, will you? I think they're all mine.

TONY *takes the books from* DAVID *and kneels at the trunk and begins to pack them. Enter* MARGOT. *She motions to* JAMES *who exits hurriedly.*

MARGOT. David, I simply had to come and I say I'm sorry.

At the sound of her voice, they turn and face her, then settle down into their positions at the table.

I suppose you guessed it was I who rang up the Proctors last night... Perhaps I shouldn't have come, but I felt I had to say how sorry I was... I honestly didn't know what I was doing, and when I realised what it would mean to you, it was too late... I suppose they've sent you down? Do believe me, David, I'll never forgive myself for this as long as I live.

They take no notice of her.

Please say something.

DAVID. Tony, I think this book belongs to you. It's got no name in it, and I don't remember buying it.

MARGOT. I wonder if you realise what it means to me to come here like this, to humiliate myself – to ask you to try and understand, David – at least believe I'm sorry.

DAVID. Tony, throw me that book with the red cover, will you. I think that one is mine.

TONY *throws him the book.*

MARGOT. I see – I was wrong to come here – Oh, I've always thought you were hard and cruel, but I never dreamt you could be as inhuman as this. You make me feel glad I did it. (*Working herself into a fury.*) Glad you're being sent down... Glad – glad – glad and I'd do it again.

She sinks down on the sofa and sobs.

TONY. I can't stand this.

TONY *moves to the door. As he passes* MARGOT, *she catches his hand and he stands like a statue with his back to her.*

MARGOT. Tony – at least *you* believe I'm sorry. You believe I love you.

TONY. You're just being theatrical. If you loved me you could never have done this.

MARGOT (*catching at a chance of being heard*). But you don't understand. I didn't realise what I was doing. I waited for you last night – and you never came. The first time, Tony, that you've never come to me. I knew it was David who prevented you.

TONY (*turning to her*). Nobody could have prevented me if I'd wanted to.

MARGOT (*a little more humbly*). Advised you, perhaps, and I – I lost my head and –

TONY. And ruined a man's career for spite.

MARGOT. Oh, no, it wasn't spite –

TONY. What was it then?

MARGOT (*slowly*). Perhaps you won't understand when I tell you it was – love.

TONY. No, I don't understand.

DAVID. I think I do now, Tony. (*To* MARGOT.) Let's forget all about last night, Margot. I don't think it was your fault any more than mine. Don't blame yourself too much for anything that's happened... Wasn't it unbelievable? Tony's only a boy. We're just the two unlucky people in his first episode. It's something we must both get over.

MARGOT. Oh, you'll both get over it. I suppose I will too. But Tony meant something more in my life than you ever realised, more than I realised myself. That's why I was fighting to keep him, but what you said to me once was right, you're impregnable. Perhaps I've been very foolish... I didn't mean to bring any unhappiness into your lives.

DAVID (*kindly*). You brought a lot of happiness to Tony – that's something to remember. Let's forget the rest.

TONY *turns away, a little embarrassed.*

MARGOT (*going to* DAVID). I'm glad you're Tony's friend.

DAVID (*taking her hand*). That makes up for a lot.

MARGOT. May I say goodbye to him?

DAVID. Tony?

TONY. Yes, David.

DAVID. Margot's waiting to say goodbye to you.

DAVID goes to the table, kneels by the trunk and picks up some books. He wants to be out of the picture. TONY comes to MARGOT. They kiss. It is a kiss of farewell. TONY gently releases her and goes to the door and opens it for her to pass out. Exit MARGOT. TONY closes the door after her.

(*Without looking up.*) Has she gone?

TONY. Yes – she's gone.

The tension between the two boys is very great. DAVID pretends to go on with his packing, but watches TONY from the corner of his eye. TONY crosses to gramophone and puts the needle down to start it without looking to see what record is in. As the gramophone starts, he goes to get a drink. The record on the gramophone is the 'signature tune' of the play, and as TONY realises it, he puts his drink down and crosses and changes the record to a lively jazz tune. This done, he crosses to the window and looks out as if to see the last of the disappearing MARGOT. DAVID remains at the trunk. He realises all that is passing through TONY's mind, but not a word is said.

The curtain slowly falls.

The End.